SLAVISTIC PRINTINGS AND REPRINTINGS

edited by

C. H. VAN SCHOONEVELD

Indiana University

280

SELECTED LETTERS
OF
EVGENIJ BARATYNSKIJ

by

G. R. BARRATT

Carleton University, Canada

1973

MOUTON

THE HAGUE · PARIS

Printed in The Netherlands by Mouton & Co., The Hague

For my Parents

PREFACE

This is a book intended both for those with specialized interests in the period dealt with (1814-1844), and for those more generally interested in the poetry and literature of nineteenth-century Russia. By direct extension, the letters given here have been selected with two overlapping aims: to present, for those who know something of Baratynskij's life and work, letters that reflect his literary outlook and in which are well expressed his views on works by his contemporaries; and to make available to the broader English-speaking public letters that will enable them to form a true impression of his life and character, interests and literary opinions. Already, one problem facing the editor of any author's letters has been solved – there are no laundry bills, no orders to restauranteurs, not even one scribbled note to a horse-seller among the present selection. Also excluded, although not without some soul-searching, are numerous childish letters to aunts, uncles and parents, and several letters of – in Lukacs' phrase – "unrevealing content", notably to literary critics and acquaintances. By no means all the extant letters of Baratynskij, it must be emphasized, are in this volume; although more than half the letters gathered between 1908 and 1915 by M. L. Gofman, editor of the Imperial Academy of Sciences' edition of Baratynskij's works (1914-1915), were lost in the disturbances of the October Revolution, almost one hundred survive. Here, an attempt is made specifically to include letters which, first, cast light on Baratynskij's aesthetic, throwing into relief his literary demands and personal shortcomings as a poet, and, second, provide or supplement such biographical information as is the common stock of modern literary history.

The letters reflect different periods of Baratynskij's life – his schooldays in the capital, his semi-exile in Finland as a result of an adolescent theft, the early years of his marriage, the time of his journey to France and Italy. I have found no more suitable way of presenting them than chronologically.

I have, of course, endeavoured always to preserve the sense of the original. That is a ground-rule the infringement of which results in death by the critic's fire. Style, however, is never a negligible factor in the translation of personal correspondence, and in Baratynskij's case it has loomed large. As a letter-writer, even allowing for the natural differences of tone in letters to such varied individuals as parents and potential patrons, close friends and mere acquaintances, his style has a basic unity. It is peculiar to himself. Some effort has been made, therefore, to convey not only the various rhythms and styles used at different times and with quite varying purposes (the official, the consciously literary in late adolescence, and the intimate), but also the quality that invests most of the letters and all the later ones. That quality is one of measure and constraint. Even the most casual of Baratynskij's letters has characteristic dignity, and it is that dignity, perhaps, that best distinguishes his correspondence from that of Puškin, Del'vig or Jazykov. Baratynskij made marginal use of puns, rarely indulged in word-play and practically never employed the folk-expressions that bespeckle Puškin's private letters. Even colloquialisms are not common. It was Baratynskij's peculiar skill, having placed these limitations on himself, to write in an engaging, fluent and often lively manner. Because of his self-discipline in these respects, there have been few purely verbal problems to overcome in the translation. Whenever the meaning of idioms or, more especially, allusions is not clear immediately, however, explanations are given in the notes.

For names of Russian individuals, the Harvard System of transliteration has been used consistently with two exceptions. First, Alexander and Peter have been given in their English forms, instead of Aleksandr and Petr; second, place names have been given in the usual English or Anglicized forms, thus: Moscow, Petersburg, Paris. (Following the Russian custom even of the 1820s, Petersburg is deprived of its saint.) Gel'singfors has been preferred to the more modern Helsinki because it was the accepted form in the period concerned here. The same system of transliteration has been used not only for names of Russian origin but also for Baltic Germans, and for the Russified or those commonly thought of as Russian (Bulgarin, Gogol').

All dates are according to the Julian calendar, which was used in Russia until 1918 and by which, as Baratynskij remarks (Letter 70), Russia was twelve days younger than the Western European nations.

TEXTS

The texts given here have been translated from a variety of sources, and detailed information of each letter's provenance and place of original publication is provided in the relevant notes. I have been fortunate enough to inspect the original manuscripts of some thirty of the letters in the archives of Puškinskij Dom (Leningrad) and of *CGALI* (Moscow). When such inspection has not been possible, as in the case of the majority of these letters, the basic texts employed have been the 1884 (Kazan') edition of Baratynskij's works and the 1951 edition of his verse, *poèmy*, prose and letters. In the latter case, letters have then been checked against the versions printed in the literary journals or almanacs given by name. Also included are six youthful letters first published in my article "E. A. Baratynskij; Unpublished Correspondence", of 1969 (*Canadian Slavonic Papers*, XI, 1, 108-119).

THE LETTERS PROPER

The complete text of each letter is translated in full, including not only the body of the letter but also the place and date of writing (where available), the initial greeting, complimentary close and signature, even though part of this information may be duplicated in the headings. Literal translations are given of pieces of verse quoted in letters, as of original pieces incorporated in them. The original line patterns, however, are preserved. As might be expected in a collection of over seventy letters, there are several words or passages that are far from clear, either because they were hurriedly written or, more often, because the note-paper, fragile with age, makes reading difficult. When words or groups of words are missing, or were deliberately erased by Baratynskij himself, the hiatus is indicated by square brackets. If pertinent, a note is provided. Where I have failed to decipher the original, or found the original to be less clear than its published form suggests, rounded brackets are used.

As was customary in Baratynskij's class and milieu, many of his letters contain words, phrases and even, on rare occasions, whole sentences in languages other than Russian, notably French and Old Church Slavonic. In this edition, the whole content of each letter is translated into English.

I have resisted the temptation to make Baratynskij's letters 'easier to read' by smoothing out inconsistences, correcting the original punctuation and orthography of certain early letters, and so forth. Nor, except when unavoidable, have other so-called improvements been adopted. Long and complex sentences are not broken up into their component parts. The paragraphing and Baratynskij's own abbreviations have also been preserved throughout.

From first to last, Baratynskij's letters show him to be an active and most conscientious correspondent. Even under the sun of Naples, he finds time to send his impressions of Italians and Italian life to N. V. Putjata in Russia. The letters reflect his literary development from the time of blatant imitation and conscious apprenticeship to the years of personal and artistic maturity. They both throw light on Baratynskij's own life, work and interests and, by reflecting his connections with the leading literary figures of his time, create a broad and interesting picture of Russian literature in its Golden Age.

The letters are, together with his articles and introductions, the best of all sources for those who wish fairly to estimate Baratynskij's attitudes both toward literature (and poetry in general) and his own poetry. His many comments and critiques on the works of his contemporaries and writers of the recent past are so just that no subsequent critic has been able to ignore them altogether in assessing his work and place in Russian literary history. Nor, happily, was Baratynskij entirely reticent about his own work. While he seldom speaks of any work while it is being written, he not infrequently gives his opinion of its strengths and weaknesses once it is published; while he does not defend the merit of his own *poèmy*, he gives his reasons for scorning his critics. Never, however, does one see reflected in his correspondence the agonies of indecision, of re-writing and destroying and re-writing; that part of the creative process he regards as private. Rather than show the slow development of any single piece, with all the accompanying strains, the letters reflect the circumstances of Baratynskij's life, his mood and state of mind while they were written, re-written and published.

Except in the cases of Hugo and Barbier, whom he considered "men who took the wrong sled" and viewed "as the sober view the drunk", Baratynskij always showed himself open to new literary currents, as to the tastes of the day, in form and subject-matter. Never, on the other hand, was he prepared to pander to that changing public taste, nor is anything clearer in his letters than his scorn of those who wrote "to order", and of "the Aristarchi of the Russian Parnassus" who dictated the fashion in literature. His sarcasm at the expense of professional critics was sharp. When he judged the works of others, it was in a disinterested way; unable to meet the requirements of political and social relevance, his own work would be damned in his own lifetime by Belinskij. He, on the other hand, judged the poetry of his contemporaries by its own standards. There was no petty selfishness, no effort to set off his own work to advantage. He praised Žukovskij generously even when his own elegiac verse was in no way inferior to "the teacher's". When he condemned Rousseau, he gave adequate reasons for doing so – by his canon, Rousseau was "one-sided", no more than "a poet of self", while the true object of art is to express the whole human condition in its complexity. He assumed that fellow-writers wanted his honest opinion of their works, and expected the same of them.

Baratynskij saw himself as a family man and a poet, and nothing more. Outside the field of literature, indeed, his contacts were not many. Unlike Puškin, he was acquainted with few figures of importance in the government or high society. He was not even a particularly perspicacious or interested observer of the social and political developments of Russia or the West in his own day. As his opposition to the notion of full Polish independence typified that of the liberal gentry of which he was a member, so, too, did his tempered enthusiasm for Liberal ideas and his unfeigned pleasure on hearing of a measure that would lighten the serf's harsh lot. Yet always he was liberal, and not a Liberal. Never was he prepared to *act* to effect those high ideals of equity and universal justice with which he sympathized.

Although he had a place in the society of Petersburg and Moscow by birth and education (his mother had been fraülein to the old Empress), he chose to make his life in neither. Three princes attended his burial in the Alexander-Nevskij Monastery in Petersburg; yet he considered himself "not a society person". He was never at the hub of Russian social and political life, nor did he wish to be so. Instead, he sought the peace and isolation of the countryside, and those needs, which never left him, are faithfully reflected in his letters. His ideal was bucolic; in his fantasies, he sat by his own hearth surrounded by his friends and family, and there was no smoky town on the horizon. In literary terms, conversely, it was hardly possible to be nearer the centre of activity than he. Coming to Petersburg in 1818, he had soon made the acquaintance of not only Puškin and Del'vig, Pletnev and Kjuxel'beker, but also several major figures of an older generation. Later, in Moscow, he met Vjazemskij, Odoevskij, Kireevskij. There were few Russian writers of standing with whom he was not, by the 1830s, at least acquainted. With Del'vig and

Putjata he was related by marriage. As for his friendship with I. V. Kireevskij, a man six years his junior, it not only emphasized his deep capacity for friendship but also faithfully reflected the imperfect sympathy that existed between an aristocrat of the old stamp and the *Ljubomudry*, or Lovers of (German) Wisdom. Lack of sympathy became an effective bar, in 1831, and Baratynskij parted company with a younger generation. He bitterly regretted it.

There was much in Baratynskij's outlook that was Epicurean in the true sense. He sought peace, as the highest possible bliss, and saw peace as the end of all unrest – not as positive happiness, which was "not for the sons of Prometheus". He went to great lengths to secure that peace. Thus, he declined to attack the iniquities of the Nicolaevan régime, as he refrained also from openly retorting to his critics even when criticism became harsh and personal. Thus, too, he struggled to maintain a bland, neutral position among warring literary factions of the day, both in *salons* and in contemporary journalistic circles. In both areas he failed. But he continued to desire neutrality, and that desire is echoed in a number of his letters of the early 1830s.

Baratynskij was a liberal, but not willing to act on behalf of the people. He was a patriot, but only *audibly* when outside Russia. He was, at all times, consciously and unconsciously, to the very fibre of his being, a poet; that, too, is well reflected in the letters.

Of Gofman's collection of two hundred letters by the poet, approximately half have survived. Of those now known, more than three quarters are in Russian. The remainder are in French, the language of polite society. Baratynskij was himself bilingual; but his French is the conventional, more than slightly formal language of the French-speaking Russian aristocracy. He was at home in those conventions, and used them with charm and variety. It is significant, however, that the letter in which he broke to his mother the news of his disgrace, after the 'Xanykov incident' of 1815, should have been written in Russian. Russian was always the language of his personal correspondence on matters of life and philosophy, as well as of disasters.

With seven exceptions, all written by 1825, the letters given here may be said to be personal. They are addressed to friends and relatives. The seven early letters, to Žukovskij, Putjata and A. I. Turgenev, fall in a different category. Although all three were later to become friends or, in Žukovskij's case, close acquaintances, they were strangers to the poet at the time of writing, as well as his superiors and potential helpers. The letters, as one might expect given the circumstances of their writing, are distinctly formal and correct in tone, excepting that to Žukovskij, in which, as a petitioner, Baratynskij adopts a style that veers untypically between the loose and the dramatic. In general, personal letters, which make up the greater part of this selection, show a moderately wide range of style. It is a strong characteristic of his correspondence that no space is found in it for either brash colloquialisms or (still more happily) for formal stiffness. This is not to say that there are no colloquialisms in letters by Baratynskij; it would be a strange writer indeed who dispensed with them entirely. In the main, however, idioms and Russian colloquial speech are well contained in Baratynskij's correspondence, in which extremes of every kind are noticably missing. There is no scintillating brilliance, no hint of parody; banter is absent, as are insolent and malicious comments, passion that seems to strain the leash, the quick arts of the raconteur. Neither very long nor very short (the average length of the letters is some 250 words), the letters given here show logical development of content and a balanced style. Baratynskij does not, like Puškin, flit lightly from subject to subject. Each letter gives the impression of having been considered, and outpourings are rare in the extreme. Spontaneity, on the other hand, is brightened, not dulled, by exact expression. There are few postscripts.

Never top-heavy, Baratynskij's sentence structure is often elaborate. But such elaboration is deliberate, and not the careless tacking on of frills and flourishes. Sentences comprised of four or five phrases are interspersed with comments of four or five words. The sense of balance may waver under the impetus of a rush of recollections; but never does that balance fail. The result is not a dynamic style, but a measured one. The rhythm is steady, and does not suddenly pull up or break into a cheerful gallop. There is no nervous impatience – rather a constant effort to express, fully and lucidly, ideas that are often complex and original. I have tried to reflect that sense of the deliberate in English.

With all their stylistic variety, perhaps the most characteristic quality of Baratynskij's letters is sincerity; after that, measure. At their worst, they can be ponderous – a fault exacerbated by a heavy, sometimes even archaic vocabulary. At their best, they are models of interest and construction. Always they are rewarding, as a running commentary on Baratynskij's life and work.

CONVENTIONAL AND FORMAL LETTER OPENINGS AND ENDINGS

Literal translations of formal and often heavy salutations and conclusions, such as were thought not merely normal but *de rigueur* in the period dealt with here, may seem to modern Western readers bizarre or even comic. When everyone of noble birth was "excellent" (to his correspondents), and all princes illustrious or gracious, it was a simple matter to fill up a line or two with titles. Endings, in particular, were highly conventional, and a "devoted servant" of the 1830s closely approximated to a modern "very sincere". Except when an acceptable English equivalent has eluded me, therefore (as for "respected Vasilij Andreevič", letter 6, and "true respect and perfect loyalty" in several early letters) I have tried to find such an equivalent. Yet it is dangerous to seek to improve on a text. The much-used formula: "Farewell, I embrace you" has thus been rendered literally, since Russians did embrace on meeting and a watery anglicism serves no purpose. "Yours" or "your house" has sometimes been given as "your people" or "your family"; exactly who was included in the greeting is seldom clear.

NOTES

Since this edition is intended both for those with some knowledge of Russian literature and for the simply curious, it has been thought better to tend to fullness in notes than to make brief, bare comments of uncertain value. It is hoped that the general reader will come upon sufficient facts in this volume to appreciate and understand the letters; facts are not ready-sorted and displayed for him. The convention of indicating lifespans and describing persons mentioned by a qualifying adjective or noun has been followed. For those whose interests fall specifically in the first part of the nineteenth century sources of information for each note are generally provided. Any edition of Baratynskij's letters must heavily rely on the thorough scholarship of certain Soviet scholars, notably on the fine introductions and annotations of I. N. Medvedeva, E. N. Kuprejanova and K. V. Pigarev. Still valuable are M. L. Gofman's annotations to the Academy of Sciences' (1914-1915) edition of the poet's work. But the chief debt, for the present notes, is to K. V. Pigarev, in whose *1951 edition* appear the only letters by Baratynskij yet to have been published in collected form since the October Revolution.

As well as Pigarev's edition, and those of 1869, 1884, 1914-1915, 1936 and 1957, I have of course made use of several Russian and Soviet encyclopaedias; pre-Revolutionary studies of the poet's work and of the verse of Del'vig, Puškin, Vjazemskij and Jazykov; short analytic studies by Soviet commentators; books and journals cited by Baratynskij; and, most of all, early and mid-nineteenth-century Russian journals and almanacs. All information given has, whenever possible, been checked against at least one other source.

I am much indebted to the academic staff of *Puškinskij Dom*, who placed original correspondence at my disposal, as to Professors A. K. Grigor'jan and D. E. Maksimov, of Leningrad State University, who gave valuable advice.

Ottawa, 1973

TABLE OF CONTENTS

LIST OF ABBREVIATIONS

Academy edition	*Polnoe sobranie sočinenij E. A. Baratynskogo*, 2 vols. (St.P., 1914-1915).
A. S. Puškin, 1962	A. S. Puškin, *Sobranie sočinenij v desjati tomax* (Moscow, 1959-1962).
B	*Blagonamerennyj*
CS	*Carskoe selo*
CGALI	*Central'nyj Gosudarstvennyj Arxiv Literatury i Iskusstva* (Moscow).
E	*Evropeec*
FP	First Published
MV	*Moskovskij vestnik*
MN	*Moskovskij nabljudatel'*
MT	*Moskovskij telegraf*
Muratova	*Istorija russkoj literatury XIX-ogo veka; bibliografičeskij ukazatel'*, ed. Muratova (Moscow, 1962).
NZ	*Nevskij zritel'*
NL	*Novosti literatury*
Ostaf'evskij arxiv	*Ostaf'evskij arxiv Knjazej Vjazemskix*, 6 vols., ed. V. S. Saitov (St.P., 1899-1913).
OZ	*Otečestvennye zapiski*
Puškinskij Dom	Institut Literatury Akademii Nauk SSSR (Leningrad).
PZ	*Poljarnaja zvezda*
S	*Sovremmenik*
SL	*Slavjanin*
SN	*Starina i novizna*
SO	*Syn otečestva*
SP	*Sorevnovatel' prosveščenija i blagotvorenija*
Sumerki	*Sumerki; sočinenie Evgenija Baratynskogo* (1842).
SC	*Severnye cvety*
Tatevskij arxiv	*Iz Tatevskogo arxiva Račinskix* (Petrograd, 1916).
Tatevskij sbornik	*Tatevskij sbornik S. A. Račinskogo* (St.P., 1899).
P. A. Vjazemskij, 1883	P. A. Vjazemskij, *Polnoe sobranie sočinenij*, 6 vols., ed. S. D. Šeremetev (St.P., 1883-1896).
1827 edition	*Stixotvorenija Evgenija Baratynskogo* (Moscow, 1827).
1835 edition	*Stixotvorenija Evgenija Baratynskogo*, 2 Pts. (Moscow, 1835).
1869 edition	*Sočinenija Evgenija Abramoviča Baratynskogo* (Moscow 1869).
1884 edition	*Sočinenija Evgenija Abramoviča Baratynskogo* (Kazan', 1884).
1936 edition	*Baratynskij; polnoe sobranie stixotvorenij*, 2 vols. (Leningrad, 1936). (Unless otherwise stated, all references to this

edition are to volume 1).

1945 edition	E. A. Baratynskij, *Stixotvorenija* (Moscow, 1945).
1951 edition	E. A. Baratynskij, *Stixotvorenija, poèmy, proza, pis'ma* (Moscow, 1951).
1957 edition	E. A. Baratynskij, *Polnoe sobranie stixotvorenij* (Leningrad, 1957).

1

Dear Mamma,

I cannot express the pleasure that I felt on reading your letter. My dear Mamma will come to see me in the summer, and I have nothing more to desire.[2] Ah! dear Mamma, how impatience makes the time seem long for me. There are still three months to summer, it is a long while, but in the end one must resign oneself. I am presently at my uncle's, Il'ja Andreevič,[3] Peter Andreevič[4] has not yet arrived, but we are expecting him at any

---

[1] The first five letters are taken from *spiski* by M. L. Gofman, editor of the 1914-1915 *Academy edition*, and preserved in Puškinskij Dom (Institut Russkoj Literatury Akademii Nauk SSSR), under the archive reference: R. 1, op. 2, no. 17. Gofman's copies are meticulous and legible. All five are in French. The originals were probably lost during the summer months of 1917 together with more than one hundred other letters by the poet gathered by M. L. Gofman. Other childhood letters, in original, may be found in CGALI, in the Baratynskij Archive; they are to nine different persons, including his mother, uncle Bogdan Andreevič, and sister N. A. Baratynskaja; there are also four letters to A. A. Del'vig, of 1826 and no date. See also my article, "Eight Unpublished Letters of E. A. Baratynsky", *Canadian Slavonic Papers*, XI (1969), 1, 108-119.

The present first letter, similar in style and content to Letters I and II from the invaluable *Iz Tatevskogo arxiva Račinskix*, ed. Ju. Verxovskij (Petrograd, 1916), 21-22, would seem to have been written between 1813 and 1815. The fact of Baratynskij's close knowledge of a financial transaction involving 700 roubles, as well as the tutor's humble addresses to the young master, suggest 1814 or 1815, rather than the earlier date. There is no postmark.

[2] Baratynskij entered the Petersburg *Corps de Pages* as 'a pensioner of private means' in early December, 1812. A. F. Baratynskaja continued, after the death of the poet's father in March 1810, to live on the estate of Vjažlja, in Kirsanov *uezd* of the Province of Tambov, which had been granted to her husband and brother-in-law by Paul I in December 1796.

[3] Il'ja Andreevič, youngest of the poet's three paternal uncles (1776-1837), was either living in Petersburg apart from his wife, who lived constantly at Il'inovsk, also in Kirsanov *uezd*, Tambov, or, more probably, was staying with his brother Petr. Il'ja was a Counter-Admiral in the Imperial Navy.

[4] Petr Andreevič (1772-1845) lived permanently in Petersburg, where he pursued a successful civil career, becoming a Senator and Member of the Privy Council (*Dejstvujuščij tajnyj sovetnik*). It was Bogdan (1771-?), however, who loomed largest of the uncles in Baratynskij's adolescence, and of whom he was most fond. On Bogdan's

moment. I ask you to tell Varen'ka[5] that her brothers are well, only the elder is a little sick, but that will pass. We spent the whole of yesterday together. My uncle[6] has received the 700 roubles of which you speak to me, and is very surprised that you have not learned of it, for he has since written two letters on that subject.[7] You say I must[8] not disturb myself on account of my mother, but what have I in the world more valuable than a mother, and a mother as good and affectionate as you. Ah Mamma if a son is not concerned for his mother he is no longer a son. Fedot is well, uncle has had an overcoat made for him but he has no more linen or trousers. Farewell my dear Mamma be well. I embrace my dear brothers[9] and sisters, my uncle, my aunt and I thank Aleksandra Nikolaevna for her letter.[10]

Dear Mr Boriès I thank you with all my heart for your letter:[11] it gave me great pleasure. But leave, I beg you, these base addresses of very humble servant there is nothing I hate so much as these insipid civilities. I want the title of friend. It was with that title that we left one another. Farewell my[12] old friend be well.

Eugène

---

estate of Podvojskoe, in the Province of Smolensk, Baratynskij passed the months immediately following his expulsion from the *Corps de Pages* in 1816. Admiral Bogdan had an extensive library, there was frequent company, and the crucial months passed not unpleasantly for the 'criminal'; see *Tatevskij arxiv*, 27, and I. N. Medvedeva, "Baratynskij", *Stixotvorenija* (Moscow, 1945), 5-18.

[5]   Varen'ka Kučina was a distant cousin who lived, in 1814-1815, in the Province of Smolensk, not far distant from Podvojskoe. According to S. A. Račinskij (see *Tatevskij arxiv*, 34), a number of Baratynskij's early poems, notably "Razluka", "Ropot", "Razuverenie" and "Opravdanie", were addressed to her. The last two at least would suggest that he was emotionally attached to her.

[6]   Il'ja Andreevič.

[7]   The letters have not survived.

[8]   Lit. *que je doit*. Baratynskij's French was not yet all that it might be. Other errors are *ocle*, for *oncle*, *vottre*, for *votre*, *quitez*, for *quittez*, *mo*, for *mon*, and miscellaneous faults of accent and punctuation. (*Temp* for *temps*, however, was acceptable usage at the time).

[9]   Baratynskij had three brothers, Iraklij (b. 1801), Lev (b. 1806) and Sergej (b. 1807), and three sisters, Sophie (1801-1844), Natal'ja (1810-1855) and Varvara (1810-1891). Sophie was sickly all her life and lived with her mother at Mara. Natal'ja was with Baratynskij at Artemovo in the winter of 1841, and travelled with him to Moscow in 1842 (*Tatevskij arxiv*, 67). Baratynskij was closer to her than to his other sisters.

[10] Aleksandra Nikolaevna Zajcova was one of three sisters (Avdot'ja and Nadežda being the eldest and youngest), daughters of a neighbouring landowner in Tambov, of whom A. F. Baratynskaja was particularly fond. They visited her frequently (*Tatevskij arxiv*, 33).

[11] The postscript to Giachinto Borghese, tutor to Baratynskij and to his three brothers, casts interesting light on the relationship between pupil and tutor in the early years of the century. Borghese did not, like Puškin's Beaupré, arrive with the yearly supply of oil, but probably had no pedagogical training whatever and as little money. He was immediately liked by all at Mara (Vjažlja), and the comment "*Il n'y a rien que je haisse…*" rings as true as the lengthy expressions of filial affection ring false. The affection that Baratynskij felt for his mother is not in dispute; but its expression, stylized in a consciously Gallic 'literary' manner, is unfortunate and stilted. Baratynskij did not forget his debt to the Italian expatriate on arriving in Italy in 1884 ("Djad'ke-Ital'jancu").

[12] Lit. *mo*. It is plain from this letter that relations between A. F. Baratynskaja and Il'ja Andreevič remained cordial, and that Baratynskij expected that she would shortly make a trip to visit Bogdan, at Podvojskoe.

2

no date

Dear uncle, dear aunts![1]

I hasten to wish you a happy new year and to wish you everything that it is possible to wish in it (–). Uncle[2] will not manage to write to you and bids me express all the happiness and joy that he wishes you. Annečka and Vavočka are not writing to you because today they are at the pension.[3] Farewell dear uncle and aunts, I hope that you will pass the new year as merrily as possible and wish you all possible happiness. I remain your humble servant and nephew,

Evgenij Baratynskij

[1] The aunts are the two sisters of Bogdan Andreevič, Katerina and Mar'ja. Where they were living is not clear. There is no postmark, but the style and content suggest that the note was written in Petersburg in 1814 or 1815. Baratynskij was attached to his paternal aunts; "Madrigal' požiloj ženščine…" (1819) was dedicated to Mar'ja, the elder of the two (1771-1844), who was clearly devoted to "Bubin'ka", as she called her nephew in childhood (see *Academy edition*, vol. 1, 212). It is known that in 1816, Mar'ja was living near Podvojskoe, so could visit Bogdan easily. Baratynskij wrote in that year (*Tatevskij arxiv*, 28), "*J'ai passé deux jours chez ma tante Marfa A., qui me caresse vraiment comme un fils.*" Katerina (1783-1844) remained unmarried, and lived on her brother-in-law's estate of Mar'inka, near Vjažlja. (Mar'ja's married name was Pančulidzeva). Mar'ja received the better education of the two, at the Smol'nyj Institute – a fact that suggests that the family were far from impoverished even after Abram Andreevič's sudden disgrace in April or May, 1798; see *Academy edition*, vol. 1, XIX.

[2] Petr Andreevič.

[3] The unspecified pension was in Petersburg. It is conceivable that the "dear aunts" might have included Ekaterina Fedorovna Čerepanova, a maternal aunt who also lived constantly at Mara, and who might well, therefore, have joined a new-year gathering at Podvojskoe.

3

May 30[1]

I (Beginning missing) ... and I thank her for her letter I kiss the hands of my uncle and aunts, my compliments to Mr Boriès tell Varvara Niko-laevna that I will write to her by the next post but have not time at present.

Your Eugene

Dear brothers and sisters,[2]

I have not time[3] to write much but something is always worth having. I love you very much and (–) do not forget you learn our comedy well so that my aunt is well satisfied with you when she arrives[4]. I would ask you, dear Sophie[5] and dear Alexandrine,[6] to (–) these shoes that I am sending you. I hope that you wear my spurs dear uncle farewell dear friends my brothers and sisters remember the drover's table and his children[7] and me.

Egene

[1]   This letter, or pair of notes, also dates from 1814-1815, and was written, presumably, in the *Corps de Pages*.

[2]   The second brother, Iraklij, pursued a military career no less brilliant than his father's. A cavalry officer and adjutant to Field-Marshal Count P. X. Wittgenstein, C-in-C of the Second Army, he was awarded a golden sword engraved *Za Xrabrost'* ('For Valour') after actions in the Turkish wars of 1828-1829. He made a brilliant marriage with the wealthy and beautiful Princess Anna Davydovna Abamelik, later to translate Lermontov and Puškin into English (see A. D. Baratynskaja, *Translations from Russian and German poets by a Russian lady*, Baden-Baden, A. von Hagen, 1878). In 1840 he began a second career as a government administrator. He became a Senator and, in 1846, Governor of Kazan'. Baratynskij was not close to him in later years. Nor was he close to Lev who, as a result of an unfortunate *affaire du coeur*, was obliged to retire from the army prematurely. He withdrew to his estate of Ljubiči, and lived the life of a *lišnij čelovek à la* Pavel Kirsanov.

   Far closer to Baratynskij was Sergej, the youngest of the brothers. Sergej was "of a genial nature, lively, passionate, endowed with the most varied abilities" — according to S. A. Račinskij, who had no reason to flatter his memory. He studied medicine in Petersburg, returned to Mara and built, in one wing of the house, a small field-hospital, from which he treated the population of the province free of charge. He also constructed a chemical laboratory and made fireworks for his nephews. As an architect, he designed and built a castle and summer-house in the grounds, in which, under his guidance and with instruments that he had turned, the family gave performances of Italian operetta, notably of Donizetti's "Anne Bolyn". He travelled widely, visiting London, and transported the fox-hunting habit to Tambov. He was subject to bouts of chronic depression (see Letter 61).

[3] Lit. *tems*.
[4] Probably Mar'ja Andreevna, who did not live near Mara and so would 'arrive' from a distance and know nothing of the theatrical preparations. The comedy itself, which Baratynskij seems to have written with some degree of assistance from his brothers and sisters, has not survived. Already, Mara was the scene of various family-*cum*-cultural activities. The chemical laboratory, hospital and summer-house have been mentioned; further on this centre, see B. N. Čičerin, "Iz moix vospominanij", *Russkij Arxiv* (1890), 501-517.
[5] Sophie, Baratynskij's eldest sister, was already weakly.
[6] Alexandrine was Baratynskij's cousin, eldest daughter of his mother's sister, Anna Fedorovna Lukaševiča. In 1814, Alexandrine was Sophie's companion at Mara; she had no fortune, and later became governess of a ladies' institute in Kiev (see *Tatevskij arxiv*, 25). From the letter it is plain that she was regarded as one of the family.
[7] The allusion is not clear. Possibly *buveur* was intended (in place of *bouveur* drover), which would suggest a print or painting of moral intent; but there is no basis for this hypothesis. Once again, the orthography is original.

4

no date[1]

Dearest Mamma,

I have just received your letter and cannot express the joy that I felt on seeing that you love me as before and forgive me my faults. Truly I needed that comfort.[2] It reconciled me with myself, and it is clear to me now how greatly preferable that comfort is to all the pleasures of dissipation.[3] I spend each holiday at my uncle's, who has been so good as to hire a teacher of mathematics for me, and I have already made quite considerable progress. May I presume to repeat my request to you concerning the naval service? I beg this kindness of you, dear Mamma. My

[1] The letter was first printed, in its original French, in the *1869 edition*, 403-407. A Russian translation immediately followed it (504-506), and was reprinted in *Tatevskij arxiv*, 36-37. The date appears to be 1815, possibly early 1816.
[2] Exactly what faults Baratynskij has in mind is not plain; it is clear, however, that the fateful events of 1816 are imminent or have started. It has been suggested by K. Pigarev that A. F. Baratynskaja (1776-1852) was "a passionate and despotic woman" (see *Muranova, muzej-usad'ba imeni F. I. Tjutčeva*, Moscow, 1948, 19). Certainly, on the death of Abram Andreevič in 1810 she devoted her considerable energy to the task of educating four sons. The estate was allowed to run down. There is no evidence of a despotic woman, however, despite Baratynskij's later admission to N. V. Putjata (*1951 edition*, Letter 13), that he yearned for independence and was surly and unhappy. Relations do not seem to have been abnormally strained in 1815-1816, still less three years later (see following letter). In later years, too, relations were cordial (see letter 6).
[3] Baratynskij speaks somewhat grandiloquently of debauch that was, one suspects, one-third real, two-thirds imagined.

interests which (you say) are so dear to you absolutely demand this.[4] I
know how hard it must be for you if I would enter such a dangerous
service. But do you know of any place on earth, even away from the
ocean's sphere, where a man's life is not subject to a thousand dangers,
where death may not steal a son from his mother, father, sister? Everywhere the least puff may destroy this feeble spring that we call life.[5] No
matter what you say, dearest Mamma, some things depend on ourselves –
others are controlled by Providence. Our actions, our thoughts depend
on us; but I cannot allow that our deaths depend on a choice of service
on dry land or on the sea. Why! is it really possible that fate, which has
fixed an end to my life, can execute its sentence on the Caspian Sea but
cannot strike me in Petersburg? I beg you not to oppose my wish, dear
Mamma. I cannot serve in the Guards; they are too well protected. In
times of war they do nothing, but remain in a state of shameful inactivity.
And will you call that life? No, unbroken calm cannot be called life.[6]
Believe me, dear Mummy, one can grow accustomed to anything except
inaction and boredom.[7] I would even prefer unhappiness in its full sense
to an imperturbable calm. At least a deep, live sensation would seize me,[8]
at least consciousness of my misfortunes would bear witness to my
existing. I feel, indeed, that I always need something dangerous and that
it should engross me – otherwise I am bored. Picture to yourself, dear
Mamma, a fearful storm, and me, standing on the deck, as though com-
manding the enraged ocean, a plank 'twixt me and death, sea monsters
marvelling at the wondrous craft – the product of human genius, which
rules the elements. Afterwards I should write to you, as often as I could,
about everything fine that I saw. And just think, dear Mamma, we shall

[4] Lit. 'insistently, persistently'.
[5] The philosophical strain is strong in Baratynskij's adolescent letters. Often, as here,
images are reminiscent of those used by Voltaire, whom Baratynskij twice mentions in
letters of 1816 (see *1884 edition*, 492, 93). Life is "this feeble spring"; humanity is "a
pullulating antheap". No doubt Petr Andreevič was somewhat surprised on learning
from his nephew that "all the undertakings of joy and sadness" are "comic, when the
ardent passions of youth cease to blind experienced old age", and on reading Baratynskij's apologies for writing something "not in keeping with his years" (*ibid.*, 493).
[6] A prophetic comment. Finland and exile would be the realization of Baratynskij's
worst adolescent fears — of enforced idleness. Subsequently, irrationally rationalizing
his personal circumstances, he would consistently praise peace (*pokoj*) as the greatest
possible bliss; see "Bokal" (1840) or "Mudrecu" (1839).
[7] That Baratynskij never grew accustomed to boredom is plain from his commercial
enterprises at Muranovo and Kajmary, the Èngel'gardts' estate near Kazan'. As well
as forestry and the marketing of wheat, a brick-factory engaged his willing attention
after 1840; see *1936 edition*, vol. 1, CIV. He was quite prepared, moreover, to travel
across France, Germany and Italy in the last months of his life.
[8] *Živoe čuvstvo...*

see each other not in five years' but in two years' time. In two years, dear Mamma, I shall embrace you and look at you and talk to you! Dear Mummy, do you appreciate my joy? Can you remain indifferent to it? I cannot believe that. Even should fate dictate that I die after a few years at sea, I should have had the chance to see you and would have delighted in that happiness. So, dear Mummy, I hope that you will not refuse me this favour. Do not a few moments of happiness, of joy, recompense a long series of wearying years? You say that you are very pleased with my leaning to intellectual activities; but admit that there is nothing more laughable than the youth who is a pedant and considers himself an author because he has translated two or three pages[9] from Florian's *Estelle* (with thirty spelling mistakes and a pompous style that he thinks picturesque); who is convinced that he has the right to criticize everything, not being of an age yet to evaluate the qualities by which he is carried away, nor yet to be inspired by them; simply because others go into ecstasies over them he rapturously extols them, never, however, having so much as read them. And I, too, have this fault, dear Mamma, and am trying to shake it off. I have often eulogized *The Iliad* although I read it in Moscow and at such an early age that not only was I not inspired by its beauty – I was unable even to understand its content. I heard that everyone was enraptured by it, and showered praise on it like a monkey. I know some who do not trouble themselves to think, but who allow the common view to form their opinion, and these people, not excluding my honourable self, are very like automatons, set in motion by springs hidden in their bodies. This is an extremely long letter and I fear I have wearied you too much already.

Farewell, dear Mamma, God grant that we meet soon. I remain, by custom, your obedient servant, by instinct, your dutiful, affectionate and grateful son.

PS. Please send me a towel, for I have only two left.

---

[9]   Lit. *stranički* 'little pages'.

5

no heading   no date[1]

I did not send you my address because I myself did not yet know where I
should lodge – we have just taken quarters with Mr Ščlečtinskij[2] (–) three
very handsome rooms that we have yet to furnish, but furnishings are
cheap here – note the address: in Semenovskij Polk, the house of the
coffee-seller Eževskij. He is a good old man who knew my father at
Gatčina.[3] He relates all kinds of tales to me and all manner of anecdotes,
which I hear with a great deal of pleasure.[4] He has a wife and tolerably
well educated daughter who speaks poor French, plays the piano in the
manner of our Oščenka goddesses,[5] has read a few novels by Mrs Rad-
klif[6] and complains that nothing in the world answers her heart's sublime
affections. All this little society is rather agreeable. I spoke to you in my
last letter of a Mme Erssgross whose acquaintance I have made, well she
is a woman of gold. She is extremely learned – that is to say she knows
more than I do, so everyone judges. She plays the harp divinely, reads a
great deal, loves painting, poetry and literature and even has[7] her own
opinions on all the arts – I discuss everything with her: friendship, love
and intrigue, epicureanism, platonism, stoicism, all this comes up for
argument.[8] I shall visit her every afternoon so long as I do not grow
bored there; it must be admitted that, awaiting better, she is a divine
woman. I am moved even to love her but do not fear anything on my
account. I am too foolish to commit a serious folly. Perhaps you will find
all this a little cavalier? Think all that you will of me, but remember too
that I love you with all my heart. Madame E. (–) me actually last night[9]
she plays the Tyrolienne on the harp – and do you know her figure even
resembles it a little!

[1]   Written in Petersburg, 1818-1819. On returning to the capital, intending to serve as a
foot-soldier and so win the Tsar's lost favour, Baratynskij lived first with Petr Andreevič,
later with Del'vig. The address mentioned here is celebrated in a poem written jointly
by Del'vig and Baratynskij, "Tam, gde Semenovskij Polk..." (1819); see *Academy
edition*, vol. 1, 200. It appears that Del'vig had not yet moved in when this letter was
written.
[2]   Ščlečtinskij, of whom nothing is known, was the landlord – not a fellow tenant.
[3]   Abram Andreevič had been commander of the Gatčina, Pavlovsk and Kameno-
Ostrov (palace) units under Pavel Petrovič, 1794-1798, whose confidence he had won by
efficient administration and sheer affection for Pavel's 'Prussian' brigades; see "Zapiso-
čki Pavla Petroviča k Abramu Andreeviču Baratynskomu, 1794-1797", *Russkij arxiv*
(1870), 1439-1441. The granting to him of the estate of Vjažlja, with 2000 souls, his
marriage to a *fräulein* of the Empress Mar'ja Fedorovna, Aleksandra Fedorovna
Čerepanova, and his disgrace for unknown or imagined failings, all occurred within

eighteen months (December, 1796-May, 1798); see *Academy edition*, vol. 1, XVII and *1936 edition*, vol. 1, XXXV.

⁴ Unfortunately, he did not see fit to record those anecdotes.

⁵ I can find no reference to the goddesses of Oščenka. They are, perhaps, sisters known to Baratynskij and his family for their musical pretensions.

⁶ The novels of Mrs Radcliff (Baratynskij's spelling betrays his total ignorance of English) were widely read in Russia in the opening years of the last century, particularly by women of gentle birth and few pressing engagements; on this, M. Lerner has interesting comments, *Zven'ja*, 1935, no. 5, 72.

⁷ Baratynskij's own pretensions to learning are piquant. He is surprised that any woman should know as much as he; his comment on Eževskij's daughter's poor French, too, is thrown into relief by his own curious orthography.

⁸ Lit. *tout cela se met sur le tapis.*

⁹ ... *m'a très vivement (-) hier au soir.* The fact of Baratynskij's having a liaison with an older woman of good social standing is no more interesting than the fact of his relating (admittedly vague) details to A. F. Baratynskaja. He seems almost to use his mother as a *confidante.* Certainly, he is aware of acting in the best Western tradition of society living (see Constant's *Adolphe*). He would be sorry, it appears, if his mother did not think "all this a little cavalier".

6

To V. A. Žukovskij   (Oct.-Dec., 1823; Ročensal'm)[1]

You put me under a strange obligation, respected Vasilij Andreevič; I would say a difficult one, if I knew you less well. But I am certain that on asking me for this story of my dissolute life you were prepared to hear it

[1] Taken from *Russkij Arxiv* (1868), bk. 1, 147-156. In that journal the names of Xanykov and Kristofovič are given by introductory letters only; here they are expanded. The version, with occasional changes of punctuation, was reprinted in the *1951 edition*, 463-469. The letter was written at Žukovskij's request. Žukovskij had already taken an interest in Baratynskij's case, and two of the four letters that he wrote in that connection to the Minister of Public Education, Prince A. N. Golicyn, may be found in *Russkij Arxiv* (1868), bk. 1, 156-160 ("Pis'ma Žukovskogo k A. N. Golicynu"). Further on this, see Žukovskij, V. A., *Sobranie sočinenij v 4 tomax*, vol. 4 (Moscow, 1960), 581-583.

This letter casts an interesting light both on the 'Xanykov incident' itself and on Baratynskij's attitude towards it and its consequences. As was pointed out by N. E. Maksimov ("E. A. Baratynskij po bumagam pažeskogo Ego Imperatorskogo Veličestva korpusa", *Russkij Arxiv*, 1870, bk. 2, 201-207, 638-645), the letter contains numerous factual errors. Baratynskij was writing *à thèse*, with the strength of his case in mind, and Žukovskij would be a powerful protector. He did not, for example, following his expulsion from the *Corps de Pages*, "mope in various Petersburg pensions for a year"; he passed the time at Mara and at Podvojskoe. At the time of the incident he had reached his sixteenth birthday and was not, as he claimed, "a fifteen-year-old". Xanykov and Krenicyn maximus, moreover, were fifteen in January 1816, while Priklonskij major was fourteen. Most striking of all, however, is the distortion of his treatment at the hands of tutors in the *Corps*. Reports signed by Staff-Captain Kristofovič and Captains Mancev and Denisov do not bear out the allegation that so unbending was Kristofovič's

with that condescension to which, perhaps, I have a right through my readiness to make a confession that shows me in a rather disadvantageous light.

In my destiny there was always something especially unfortunate, and this serves as my chief and general justification: everything worked in unison to destroy my good qualities and develop those productive of harm. It is a curious chain of events and impressions that turned me, truly, from a very good boy into an almost perfect good-for-nothing.[2]

At the age of twelve, I entered the *Corps de Pages*, my mother's tears and final instructions vivid in my memory and firmly resolved to carry them out to the letter and, as they say in a boys' school,[3] to serve as an example of diligence and good conduct.

The chief of my house was then a certain Kristafovič (he is now deceased, and it is a misfortune that he was not then), a man limited in everything except his passion for wine. He disliked me at first glance, and treated me as a first-class trouble-maker from the first day of my entering the corps... Affectionate toward other boys, he was particularly gruff with me. His unfairness embittered me: children are no less proud than adults, injured pride demands revenge, and I resolved to avenge myself on him. In large, calligraphic letters (we had a rather good teacher of calligraphy) I wrote *drunkard* on a scrap of paper and stuck it on the broad back of my enemy. Unfortunately, some of my fellows had seen my prank and, as we say, told on me. I sat under arrest for three days, angry with myself and cursing Kristafovič.

---

severity after an unspecified crime that he, Baratynskij, despaired of ever being pardoned. Until 1814, Kristofovič, who was "such a good officer – and acquainted with uncle" in February 1813 (see *1936 edition*, XXXVIII), gave Baratynskij good reports. In 1814 he was "of good conduct, good disposition, not punished" (N. Maksimov, *op. cit.*, 202). By 1816, however, Baratynskij was "secretive by nature" (*ibid.*, 203). Baratynskij clearly remembered the tricks that he had played on various officers in 1823. Nor is there any evidence of huge remorse for the theft itself. There is, however, no reasonable doubt that Baratynskij felt constrained in the *Corps*. A contemporary, P. M. Daragan, recorded that the tutors' interest in their charges' progress and welfare was minimal ("Vospominanija P. M. Daragana, pervogo kamerpaža ...", *Russkaja Starina*, 1875, vol. 12, 780). Such indifference no doubt aggravated feelings of frustration and isolation. Action, which is proper to childhood, is everywhere in evidence in the Baratynskij family. Baratynskij's theft of a snuff-box and five hundred roubles is to be seen as no more than the culminating point of a long process of random reading and undisciplined conduct. The consequences of that incident would last more than a decade, in terms of general outlook, all Baratynskij's life. By the last weeks of 1823 it was quite apparent that there would be no prompt promotion, and that Baratynskij might well serve another ten years before, as an officer, he could honourably retire. Those were grounds enough, perhaps, for some distortion of the facts of the crime.

[2]   ... *soveršennym negodjaem.*
[3]   *v detskom učilišče, ...*

In reality, my first escapade did not turn me into a troublesome individual,[4] but in the eyes of my superiors I was already a scoundrel. I
received constant and often unfair insults from them: instead of giving
me every opportunity to win back their good opinion, they took away
my hope of placating them, and my wish to do so, by their inflexible
severity.

In the meantime, I was drawn to certain of my comrades also not in the
administration's favour; but I was attracted to them[5] not because they
were trouble-makers but because I felt in them (I cannot say, noticed)
finer inner[6] qualities than in the others. You know that high-spirited boys
do not fight among themselves or vex their teachers and tutors[7] because
they wish to go without supper, but because they have livelier tempera-
ments, more restless imaginations and generally more ardent feelings
than other children. Consequently, I was not yet a monster when I made
friends with those of my age who were like myself in character; but my
superiors viewed it otherwise. I played not one more trick, yet a year after
my entering the corps they regarded me almost as an enormity.[8]

What can I tell you? I still remember vividly the moment when, walking
to and fro in our recreation hall, I asked myself: shall I really be a trouble-
maker? I was carried away by the idea of disregarding everything, of
casting off all constraint; a glad feeling of freedom stirred my heart, it
seemed to me that I had acquired a new existence.

I will pass over the second year of my life in the corps: it contained
nothing remarkable; but I must speak of the third, in which occurred the
dénouement of which you know. It was our custom, after each annual
examination, to do nothing for a few weeks – a right which we had ob-
tained I know not how. At this time those of us who had money would
buy books in Stupin's dirty shop, which was immediately beside the
corps, and what books! Glorioso, Rinaldo Rinaldini, robbers in all conceivable forests and dungeons! And I, to my misfortune, was one of the
most avid readers! O, would that Don Quixote's departed nurse had
been *my* nurse! With what decision would she have cast all that robber's
rubbish into the stove, rubbish as worthless as the knightly nonsense
from which her unhappy master perished. The books that I mentioned,
and Schiller's *Karl Moor* in particular, heated my imagination; the
robber's life seemed to me the most enviable in the world, and, naturally

---

4   *šalunom* 'playful, mischievous fellow/boy, prankster'.
5   Baratynskij's need of friendship increased over the years – see letter 23.
6   Lit. 'emotional (or spiritual) qualities...' (*duševnye kačestva*).
7   Perhaps, 'tutors' (*guvernerov*).
8   Lit. 'monster' (*čudoviščem*).

restless and enterprising, I conceived the plan of forming a society of avengers, the aim of which would be to torment our superiors as much as possible. A description of our society may be amusing and diverting both in its main idea, taken from Schiller, and in its other, completely childish details. There were five of us. We met in the attic each evening, after supper. According to our agreement we ate nothing at the common table, but bore away thence all the comestibles that we could carry in our pockets and then feasted at liberty in our refuge. There, too, we would all lament our fate and think up tricks of various kinds that we would later resolutely put into effect. Sometimes our teachers would find their hats nailed to the windows on which they had laid them, sometimes our officers would go home with their scarves trimmed.[9] Once we poured ground spanish fly into our inspector's snuff-box, as a result of which his nose swelled up; I cannot narrate all that we did. Having devised a trick, we chose the performer by drawing lots, and he alone would answer for it should it fail; but I usually took upon myself, as the leader, the most daring tricks.

Some time later, we received one more colleague into our society, (to my misfortune), viz. the son of that Chamberlain who, I think, is known to you, both to my own and to his regret. For a long time we had noticed that he had rather too much money about him; it seemed improbable to us that his parents gave a fourteen-year-old boy 100 or 200 roubles a week. We entered into his confidence and learnt that he had fit a key to his father's bureau, where currency bills lay in large piles; he took a few from it each week.

Having gained his secret, we of course began to use his money too. Our garret suppers became far more tasty than before: we ate sweets by the pound; but this blissful life did not last long. The mother of our comrade, who then lived in Moscow, fell dangerously ill and wished to see her son. He was granted leave and, as a mark of his zeal, left the unfortunate key with me and his relative, (Xanykov): "Take it, it will come in handy," he said to us with the most touching feeling and, indeed, it came in too handy!

Our friend's departure cast us into despondency. Farewell, pies and pastries – we had to renounce everything. But that was too much for us: we had already accustomed ourselves to luxury, and ingenuity was needed; we thought and schemed.

I must tell you that a year before this I had unexpectedly come to know the celebrated Chamberlain. That chance belongs to the chances in my

---

[9]   Lit. 'with clipped, pared, cut off scarves' (c obrezannymi šarfami).

life on the basis of which I could establish the system of predetermination. I was in hospital together with his son and, in the boredom of a lengthy convalescence, had built a small puppet-theatre. Having once been visiting my friend, he greatly admired my toy and added that he had long ago promised one like it to his little daughter, but had not yet managed to find a well-made one. I offered him mine out of generosity; he accepted the gift, showed me much kindness and asked me to visit him on some occasion with his son; but I did not take advantage of the invitation.

Meanwhile Xanykov, as a relative, was often in his house. It occurred to us that what one scoundrel can do, others can do. But X(anykov) declared that he was already suspected there because of various earlier tricks, that they would watch him, and that an associate was indispensable, who would at least occupy the servants and draw attention from himself. I had not been, but had the right to be, in the unfortunate house. I resolved to help X(anykov). Christmas approached and we were sent off to our relations. Having deceived the officers on duty, each in his own way, all five of us left the corps building and gathered at Molinari's.[10] It was decided that Xanykov and I should pay a visit to a certain person, if possible carry out our intention, and come with the reply to our comrades, who would wait for us in the shop without fail.

We each drank a glassful of liqueur for courage, and set out very cheerfully on the world's most worthless road.

Need I relate the rest? We carried out our intention only too successfully; but as a result of a fusion of circumstances of which I cannot give even myself a clear account, our theft did not remain a secret, and we were both expelled from the corps with the instruction that we might enter no service,[11] unless we should choose to serve as private soldiers.

I do not presume to justify myself; but a good-natured and, of course, over-sympathetic man, wishing to lessen my guilt in your eyes, might say: remember that he was not yet sixteen; remember that in the corps only stealing from one another is called theft, and all else is regarded as legal booty, and that among all his fellows he would have found but two or three who would have blamed him, had he succeeded in his prank;

---

[10]   A confectionery, or candy-store, by the *Corps de Pages.*

[11]   Peter the Great's system of three tables of ranks, civil, naval and military (*Tabel' o Rangax*, January 1722), was still operative in 1816. It was a relatively easy matter, moreover, to transfer from one service to another, maintaining one's rank. Implicit in Alexander's personal edict was the fact that Baratynskij might not be a guardsman, but would serve in a line regiment, i.e., would enjoy none of the prestige attached to the Guards and even to the Imperial Navy.

remember how many circumstances[12] presented the idea to his imagination, little by little. Moreover, was there not more wilfulness than anything else in his conduct? If he were truly vicious, and in consequence already rather careful and experienced, he would easily have calculated that he ran a great risk for a rather insignificant gain; nor would he have kept a kopek of the stolen money on him, but would have given it all up to his colleagues. What prompted him to such a worthless act? Youthful bravado and an imagination spoiled by bad reading. From all of which it follows only that he was more receptive than were others to impressions of all kinds and that, given another upbringing, other, more enlightened and watchful tutors, that same receptivity that served to bring about his downfall might have helped him to excel many of his fellows in all things useful and honourable.

On my expulsion from the corps, I moped in various Petersburg pensions for a year. Those who ran them, learning that I was the one about whom everyone was then talking, would not agree to keep me. A hundred times I was ready to take my life. At last I went to my mother in the country. I shall never forget my first meeting with her. She had left me fresh and ruddy; I returned dry and pale, with sunken eyes, like the son in the Gospel returning to his father. "But while he was yet at a distance, the father saw him and had compassion on him and fell on his neck and embraced him." I had expected reproaches but found only tears and an inexhaustible tenderness which touched me the more for my being unworthy of it. For four years no one had spoken to my heart: it trembled greatly at this sharp appeal to it; its light dispelled the shadows that darkened my imagination. Surrounded by the circumstances of civilian life, I came to know its terms better, and was horrified both by my crime and by its consequences. My health did not withstand these emotional changes: I fell into a high nervous fever, and could scarcely be revived.

At the age of eighteen, at my own request, I entered the Life-Guard Chasseurs as a private soldier; by chance I came to know some of our young poets, and they communicated their love of poetry to me. I do not know if my efforts for publication were good; but I know certainly that they were my salvation. After a year, on the representation of the Grand Duke Nikolaj Pavlovič, I was promoted under-officer and transferred to the Nejšlockij Regiment, in which I have already served four years.

You know how unsuccessful proved all the representations made on my behalf by my command. From year to year efforts were made for me,

[12]   Lit. 'details' (*podrobnostej*).

from year to year I was sustained by the vain hope of an early pardon; but now, I confess to you, I am beginning to despair. It is not the service, to which I have grown accustomed, that burdens me; I am oppressed by the ambivalence of my position. I belong to no condition of society whatever, although I have some name. No hopes and no pleasures are seemly in me. I am obliged to await some change in my fate in idleness, at least in spiritual idleness, and to wait, perhaps, whole years more! I do not presume to retire although, having entered the service of my own will, I must have the right to leave it when I choose; but such decisiveness may be taken as wilfulness. I only remain regretful that I freely laid chains on myself that are too heavy. Deserved unhappiness is to be borne in patience – I do not argue; but this exceeds my strength, and I begin to feel that if it should continue it will not only kill my soul but will even weaken my reason.

There, respected Vasilij Andreevič, is my story. I thank you for the sympathy that you show me; it is more than precious to me. Your kind heart is a guarantee to me that my confessions will not weaken your indulgence towards one who, by chance, has done much that is worthless, but who always by nature loved what is good.

I am yours most sincerely,[13]

Baratynskij

[13] Lit. 'With all my heart devoted to you'. For details of translations of stylized and formal endings, see p. 14.

7

To A. A. Bestužev and K. F. Ryleev   (Spring, 1824; Ročensal'm)[1]

Dear brothers Bestužev and Ryleev! Forgive my not having written to you when I sent you the remainder of my rubbish, as a decent man would have done. I am certain that you are as good-natured as I am lazy and muddle-headed. But allow me to come to the point.[2] Take the classifying

[1] Taken from *Russkaja starina*, 1888, November, 321-322.
[2] Lit. '... to approach the matter', the matter in hand (*pristupit' k delu*). The tone of this letter is very much more informal than that of the preceding one, and less stylized than that of his letters to A. F. Baratynskaja. Baratynskij met K. F. Ryleev through N. M. Konšin (1794-1865), company commander (*rotnyj komandir*) in the Nejšlotskij Foot, to which regiment Baratynskij was seconded from the Life-Guard Chasseurs in January 1820. Konšin had known Ryleev since 1820.

of my poems on yourselves, dear brothers. In my first notebook they were copied without any order, and the second book of elegies especially needs to be looked through; I would like the arrangement of my poems to suggest some links between them, and believe that they are, to a certain point, susceptible of such an arrangment. Second; let me know precisely which lines our upright censors will not pass; perhaps I may manage to rework them. Third: Del'vig writes to me that I shall receive "Les Macchabées"[3] through you, dear Ryleev; send it as soon as you can: if we're to translate, let's translate. I shall be extremely glad, by the way, if they can do without me. Fourth, O friends and brothers! try to present my children to the world in a clean dress, – books, like people, are often judged by their clothes.

Farewell, my dear friends, I wish you everything that I do not enjoy myself: pleasures, repose, happiness, – rich dinners, good wine, tender mistresses. I remain, for all the boredom of Finnish life, yours most truly,

Baratynskij

The importance of K. F. Ryleev (1795-1826) and A. A. Bestužev (1797-1837) in the Liberal or Decembrist movement in politics and literature alike need hardly be stressed. It is, in the eyes of Soviet commentators, much to Baratynskij's credit that he was closely associated, even although only briefly, with the editors of the radical almanac *Poljarnaja zvezda* (1823-1825). That association, however, was over by 1825. Never was Baratynskij actively involved in a society of *overtly* political objectives.

The poems of which Baratynskij speaks are those which finally appeared in the collection of 1827 (*Stixotvorenija Evgenija Baratynskogo*). Bestužev and Ryleev were to have published the collection (see *1936 edition*, vol. 1, 345-346), and the delay caused by the Decembrists' rising, no less than the unfortunate similarity between the collection's lay-out – in three elegiac cycles – and that of Batjuškov's *Opyty v proze i stixax* (1817), marred its prospects of success with the reading public.

[3] A tragedy by Guiraud. Also collaborating on the translation was M. E. Lobanov (see letter 24). Alexandre Guiraud (1788-1847), best known for his elegy "Le Petit Savoyard", wrote his *colourful* tragedy in 1822; the Russian translation was thus a prompt one.

8

To V. A. Žukovskij (5 March, 1824)[1]

Illness, respected Vasilij Andreevič, prevented my expressing my gratitude to you for the moving lines, which Del'vig gave me. In them you thank

[1] Taken from *Russkij Arxiv* (1871), bk. 6, 0239-0240.

me for my letter, as though *I* were obliging *you* and laboured to write it –
as if, forgetting that you alone were my benefactor, I wrote: remember
that I am unhappy and in need of comfort. Believe me, gratitude is not
irksome to me, especially gratitude to you. I loved you and wept over
your verses before I could foresee that your heart's fine qualities might
benefit me.

Such good news[2] of my affair has reached me that, to speak the truth, I
am afraid to believe it. I place my destiny in your hands, my Genius-
benefactor. You began, you will complete. You will return to me the
normal human's existence, of which I have been so long deprived that
I have even grown unaccustomed to think of myself as the same as other
men; and then I shall say, together with you: praise be to poetry, poetry
is virtue, poetry is strength; but in one poet only, in you, are all its great
qualities joined together. May your days be as splendid as your heart,
and as your poetry. Unable to think of a better wish for you, I remain, to
the depth of my heart, yours truly,

Baratynskij

[2]   The "good news" of which Baratynskij speaks seems to be that Žukovskij, aided by
A. I. Turgenev, P. A. Vjazemskij, D. Davydov, Zakrevskij and others, are continuing
their efforts on his behalf. Seven months later, he was transferred to the personal staff
of Count A. A. Zakrevskij (1783-1865), Governor-General of Finland, in which
proceeding D. Davydov played no small part; see *1936 edition*, vol. 1, LIII-LIV. The
tone of the letter was calculated to please Žukovskij who had, indeed, linked virtue
with poetry, declaring that the bad man cannot be a good poet. On his connections
with the Masonic movement and his aesthetic, see M. Ehrhard, *V. A. Joukovskij et le
Préromantisme Russe* (Paris, 1938), 4-28.

9

To N. V. Putjata   (25 May, 1824; Vil'manstrand)[1]

Baratynskij paid a call on you, wishing to present his respects and to
thank you for the concern that you so kindly show in him and in his fate.
When a better lot gives him the right to closer acquaintance with you, the
feeling of gratitude will serve as his pretext to urge your good opinion for
himself, until which time he remains your most humble servant.

[1]   Taken from *Russkij Arxiv*, 1867, bk. 2, 264, where it was first published with the
following comment by N. V. Putjata, the addressee: "In the spring of 1824, the
Finnish Governor-General, A. A. Zakrevskij, made a tour of inspection of certain
forces stationed in Finland, among them the Nejšlotskij Foot Regiment, in which

E. A. Baratynskij was serving at that time as an under-officer. The inspection took place near Vil'manstrand, on the shores of the desolate lake. I was walking along the line behind General Zakrevskij (to whom I was adjutant), when Baratynskij was pointed out to me. He was standing in the colour ranks. Baratynskij was born with the century, consequently he was then 24. He was lean, pale, and his features expressed profound depression. In the course of the review I met him, and conversed with him about his Petersburg friends. Afterwards, he called on me but did not find me at home, and left the accompanying note." (Vil'manstrand, the Finnish city of Lappeenranta, stands on the southern shore of Lake Saimaa – 'the desolate lake', 15 kilometers NW. of the present Soviet-Finnish frontier, and a mere 21 kilometers from Vyborg.)

Nikolaj Vasil'evič Putjata (1802-1877) became a lifelong friend of Baratynskij (see letters 68-72). In 1837 he married the poet's sister-in-law, Sophie L'vovna Èngel'gardt.

10

To N. V. Putjata[1]   (11 October, 1824; Kjumen')[2]

I received your letter, my dear benefactor, and do not know how otherwise to thank you for your kind suggestion than by accepting it with the liveliest gratitude. Certainly your capital would intimidate me, did you not give me hopes of finding in you a mentor and protector. Whatever awaits me in Gel'singfors, however, I count the opportunity that gives me the pleasure of passing some days with you, – and of strengthening a friendship as flattering to myself as it is pleasant, a very happy one in my life.

Not knowing your forename, I was unable to use the customary letter form in my heading; pardon me that, and be assured that it in no way weakens my true respect and complete devotion, with which, honoured Sir, I remain your most humble servant,

Baratynskij

[1] Taken from *Russkij Arxiv* (1867), bk. 2, 265. The letter is a reply to Putjata's letter, in which he informs Baratynskij of Zakrevskij's decision to allow him to join his staff, and invites him to stay in his, Putjata's, rooms. Baratynskij served in the Finnish capital from November 1824 until February 1, 1825, during which time he worked on his *poèma*, "Eda" (first published separately in 1826 together with the earlier "Piry").

[2] Kjumen' (Swedish Kymmene, Finnish Kymi) was, in 1820, a small stockaded fortress of no more than twenty buildings. It was (and is) situated on the fast-flowing river Kymijoki, surrounded by fir- and pine-forests, and was as beautiful as it was bare of civilized amenities. Baratynskij stayed in the house of his regimental commander, an acquaintance of the family, Col. Georgij Alekseevič Lutkovskij, (1763?-1831) (see "Lutkovskomu", 1824), and was treated as a member of the family. Lutkovskij, a veteran of the Napoleonic wars, was a man of liberal outlook who greatly lightened Baratynskij's position. In essence, however, that position was bound to remain a difficult one for, as he wrote to Žukovskij (letter 6), he "belonged to no situation"; he

was an officer without epaulettes, a privileged soldier without stated rights. In Kjumen', moreover, his position was ambivalent in another way. Konšin was a Liberal; so, too, would Putjata and Zakrevskij be. Yet Baratynskij, though later implicated (1821) in a secret report by V. N. Karazin to his superior, Prince V. P. Kočubej, was by no means anxious to participate in truly Liberal activities against the régime. No one in Kjumen' was more the *dvorjanin* than he.

11

To A. I. Turgenev[1]   (31 October, 1824; Gel'singfors)[2]

Your Excellency, Gracious Sir, Aleksandr Ivanovič!

If I were not deeply touched by your generous sympathy I would have no heart. I will say not a word more concerning my gratitude: you are unlike any other; there is not such a misanthropist as would not be reconciled with humanity, on meeting you among it. I could add much more, but it is my business not to judge, but to feel.

Arsenij Andreevič[3] is right in wishing to delay a little with the representation; the reason for doing so is conclusive. The following was written on the most recent memorandum about me, by the hand of the gracious monarch: Not to present again until commanded. That is why no representations were made on my behalf in Petersburg. You see that after such a decision Arsenij Andreevič can solicit for me only verbally and that he will risk an almost certain refusal, should he address a written petition. It is almost better to wait; two months will pass imperceptibly, and I am already accustomed to be patient.

Although it is your Excellency himself who deigns to inquire after my poetical work, perhaps I shall act immodestly if I tell you that I have written a small *poèma*,[4] and ask your permission to send you a copy of it.[5] My verses are all my worldly goods, and this offering would be the widow's mite.

I have the honour to remain, with true respect and perfect loyalty, your Excellency's obedient servant,

Baratynskij

[1]   There were few authors of standing in Russia, France and Germany of the first third of the nineteenth century whom Aleksandr Ivanovič Turgenev (1784-1845) had not at least met. During his visit to England, in the latter months of 1828 and early 1829, he came to know numerous British literary figures, including Thomas Moore and Sir Walter Scott. More than his brother Nikolaj even, A. I. Turgenev was a human

link between writers, poets and critics in various parts of Russia and Western Europe. His interest in Baratynskij's case, provoked, probably, by Žukovskij, became if anything more lively than Žukovskij's own.

²   This letter, written in consciously formal manner through which, however, sincerity penetrates, is taken from *Russkij Arxiv* (1871), bk. 6, 0240-0241.

³   A. A. Zakrevskij (1783-1865), Governor-General of Finland and enemy of Arakčeev

⁴   "Eda".

⁵   Baratynskij appears to have a hand-written copy in mind. At the conclusion of the letter, on the left-hand corner, are the words: "Gel'singfors. Oktjabrja 31 dnja".

12

To I. I. Kozlov   7 January (1825; Gel'singfors)[1]

So we live to see another year, my dear Kozlov; I hope that it may prove happy and full of splendid inspiration for you. I have received your *The Monk*, and have read it through with particular pleaure; some places moved me greatly. You call the work your favourite son and have good grounds for liking it: in my opinion, it is a beautiful work. The situations in it are distinctly forceful and the style is full of life and sparkles with colour; you poured your heart into it.[2] In the places where you imitate Byron you excel him, so far as I was able to judge this.[3] Four lines from "Giaour":

> But the hungry arms trembled
> And embraced only the air;
> Deceived by a dream, they
> Pressed only against his breast, –[4]

---

¹   Taken from *Russkij Arxiv* (1886), bk. 1, 187-187, where it is given in Russian. The original was in French. Ivan Ivanovič Kozlov (1779-1840) is best known for his poèma *Černec* (1825), which is loosely based on Byron's *The Giaour*, and for his many translations from Byron and Thomas Moore (as well as from Dante, Tasso, Chénier, Robert Burns, etc.). Having pursued a successful social and service career until the age 37, Kozlov was struck by paralysis in the leg. By 1821 he was blind, and over the remaining years of his life lost the powers of movement and speech. He dictated his verse to his daughter. He was highly respected by Puškin, Baratynskij and many other writers of the time. *Černec* enjoyed an enormous popular success, partly at least (as Belinskij claimed) because, like Karamzin's *Bednaja Liza*, it demanded little of its readers. See my study, *Ivan Kozlov; A study and a setting* (Toronto, A. M. Hakkert, 1972), esp. chaps. 6-7.

²   Many elements of the work recall *The Giaour* — the monk in the abbey, a death-bed confession scene, a passion that led to suicide or contemplation of it, even the dark scenaria.

³   Baratynskij read Byron in French.

⁴   Had he been able to read the English text, he would immediately have seen that

went into Russian excellently.

But the place where Byron himself would have wished to imitate you is in the ending of your *poèma*. It especially speaks to the imagination; it is filled with a special, national romanticism, and it seems to me that you are the first to have caught it. Proceed along the same path, my dear poet, and you will accomplish marvels. I will return your notebook to you next week; I am copying it out for myself, for I wish not merely to read you – I wish to study you.

I am ashamed to speak of "Eda" after *The Monk*; but for good or ill, I have finished writing it. It seems to me that I have been drawn somewhat by vanity; I did not want to go along the beaten path, and did not want to imitate either Byron or Puškin; that is why, striving to set them to verse, I plunged into various prosaic details; but I produced only rhymed prose. I wished to be original but turned out merely bizarre!

Tell our celestial Peri[5] that I am as moved by her remembering me as it is possible for an earthly envoy to be moved, that I kiss the hem of her dress, iridescent with a thousand hues, and that I know how to value her heart, which is endowed with a thousand virtues.

My affairs are going worse and worse. Living in Petersburg, you will know that my present protector[6] is retiring, which in itself will postpone my promotion by at least a year. All this inclines me to rhyming more than ever before, which proves to me that, since there is no place for me in the world of reality, my real place is in the world of poetry.

We receive almost no journals here. There is a polemical article by Kjuxel'beker in *Mnemozina*,[7] well thought out and well expressed, in my

---

(as was Kozlov's custom), the translator had 'translated' the lines from the penultimate strophe by paraphrase and by expansion. Here is the original:

> And rushing from my couch, I dart,
> And clasp her to my desperate heart;
> I clasp — what is it that I clasp?
> No breathing form within my grasp,
> No heart that beats reply to mine ...

[5] Aleksandra Andreevna Voejkova (1797-1829), wife of A. F. Voejkov, satirist, some time joint editor of *Syn otečestva*, *Russkij invalid* and *Novosti literatury*, and literary enemy, after 1826, of Baratynskij himself. Voejkova was a beauty, and sung by Žukovskij ("Svetlana") as well as by Baratynskij, ("A. A. V – oj", 1827).

[6] A. A. Zakrevskij.

[7] *Mnemozina* was published in Petersburg from 1824 to 1825 and edited by V. K. Kjuxel'beker (1799-1846) and V. F. Odoevskij (1804-1869). It showed extreme radical tendencies. There is a large body of literature on it; see *Muratova*, 76 and 400, under Sobolev, V.

view. Our Frérons[8] replied to it stupidly and distrustingly. Our journalists have become regular literary monopolists; they create popular opinion, they present themselves as our judges with the aid of their usurious machinery,[9] and there is no helping it! They are all of one party, and seem almost to have formed an alliance against all that is beautiful and honourable. A certain Greč,[10] Bulgarin[11] and Kačenovskij make up the triumvirate that governs Parnassus. You will agree that this is rather sad. We should support *Mnemozina* and we should help Polevoj's journal on its way;[12] otherwise the reputation of our works will depend on how kindly the above-mentioned gentlemen are disposed towards us.

Farewell, my dear friend. Convey my respects to Mme Kozlov and wish her a happy new year from me.

Yours, E. Baratynskij

PS. Matters have changed; the general will stay, and I am reviving.

---

[8]   The allusion is to E. Fréron (1719-1776), a minor reactionary journalist and littérateur ridiculed by Voltaire.

[9]   Lit. 'with the aid of usurious means...' (*pri pomošči svoix rostovščičeskix sredstv*). Baratynskij refers to the whole business of publishing on a commercial basis, not to physical machines.

[10]   "A certain" is derogatory. N. I. Greč (1787-1867) was editor of *Syn otečestva*. His views were 'official' and reactionary.

[11]   Faddej Benediktovič Bulgarin (1799-1859) was the object of Baratynskij's special scorn (see "Prijatel' strogij, ty ne prav...", 1827, "Čto ni boltaj, a ja velikij muž...", 1826, "Na nekrasivuju vinetku...", 1827, etc.). M. T. Kačenovskij (1775-1842), too, earned biting epigrams from Baratynskij (for example, "Ty ropšeš', važnyj žurnalist...", 1827, "Istoričeskaja èpigramma", 1829. With lapses in 1809-1814, Kačenovskij was editor of *Vestnik Evropy* from 1807 to 1830, a position which, in Baratynskij's (and Puškin's) view, he abused.

[12]   *Moskovskij telegraf* (1825-1834). The editor, N. A. Polvevoj, was a partisan of French and English romantic literature against the German opposition (represented in *Moskovskij Vestnik, Atenej, Biblioteka dlja čtenija* and, for a few short months, *Mnemozina*). Baratynskij fulfilled his intention of helping Polevoj; in 1826, he contributed three pieces to that journal, in 1827 four. Between 1827 and 1830, however, relations between Baratynskij and Polevoj, until then cordial (see letter 25), deteriorated. Polevoj's review of Baratynskij's verse collection of 1827 ("Stixotvorenija Evgenija Baratynskogo", *Moskovskij telegraf*, 1827, Pt. 17, 225-6) contained no harsh criticism. In his review of "Naložnica", on the other hand ("'Naložnica', sočinenie E. Baratynskogo", *ibid.*, 1831, vol. 38, no. 5, 235-243), there is little but censure. The introduction is too long; the question of morality in art is "outdated now"; "the characters are not developed: passions are silent", and so on. Balzac, Byron show passions – and are therefore praised.

13

To A. I. Turgenev   (25 January, 1825; Gel'singfors)[1]

Your Excellency, Gracious Sir, Aleksandr Ivanovič!

Arsenij Andreevič arrived in Petersburg on the 24th of this month, having given me all possible expectations of his patronage; but I know very well that I am indebted to your support alone for his favourable inclination. Now, when my fate hangs so decidedly on his petitioning, do not refuse to remind him of the concern with which you honour me, thereby prompting Arsenij Andreevič to fulfil his promises.

I am sending a rhymed tale[2] with this to which I referred in one of my letters. If you value not the work, but the sentiment with which I present it to your Excellency, you will be satisfied with me and will accept benevolently this insignificant mark of my lively gratitude.

With true respect and perfect loyalty, I have the honour to remain, Gracious Sir, your Excellency's most humble servant,

E. Baratynskij

This letter will be delivered to your Excellency by Adjutant Arsenij Andreevič Muxanov.[3] If, in your kindness towards me, you wish to hear of my situation in detail, he knows it intimately and will answer all your Excellency's questions satisfactorily.

[1] Taken from the *1951 edition*, 474-475, where it is given as copied from the personal collection of K. V. Pigarev.
[2] The "rhymed tale" is "Eda".
[3] Muxanov (1800-1834) was adjutant to Count Zakrevskij. He was enamoured of Aurore Šernval', daughter of the Governor of Vyborg, to whom Baratynskij addressed "Avrore Š-" (1824/5). (On this piece, written to the blue-eyed beauty who was 16 in 1824, see also *Academy edition*, vol. 1, 250.) Baratynskij wrote "Zapros Muxanovu" (1825) to the adjutant, whom he liked well.

14

To V. K. Kjuxel'beker   (Late January, 1825; Kjumen')[1]

Dear Vil'gel'm, this letter will reach you through Nikolaj Vasil'evič

[1] Taken from the original, preserved in the Baratynskij Archive, *CGALI*. The letter was delivered to Kjuxel'beker in Moscow by N. V. Putjata, who made the journey from Gel'singfors in the second week of February, 1825.

Putjata, a man who respects your talent, your temper and your heart, and who therefore wishes to make your acquaintance. We lived together in Gel'singfors for more than two months; if details concerning me should interest you, he will tell you everything that cannot be put into a letter. For a long time, too long a time, I have not written to you; but you are yourself to blame, not having given me your address. Having sent me the first part of *Mnemozina*, you did not favour me with even two lines in your own hand; despite that, I wanted to thank you for a pleasant gift, but could not since I did not know where you were living. So I decided to wait for the renewal of our correspondence until you should have grown so famous through your journal that one could address letters to you as they were once addressed to the mathematician Euler:[2] to Kjuxel'beker, Esq., in Europe. Do not be angry at this joke, old comrade, but accept my sincere greeting with a good heart.

I read your conversation with Bulgarin[3] in the third part of *Mnemozina* with real pleasure. That is how burlesque articles should be written! Your article is full of moderation, civility and, in many places, true eloquence. Your views seem to me incontestably just. They answered you stupidly and hypocritically.

Do not abandon your publication, but continue to speak the truth. I am sure that it will sell more and more; but I would advise you to make it at least a monthly. You know that journalistic literature derives its whole interest from the interest of everyday events, which it judges and discusses; let time slip by and the action is lost.

I am sending you something for your journal: I would have sent more if I had more, but you are welcome to all that I have. Farewell, dear Vil'gel'm; please reply to this; write how you are and what news you have. Our old friendship gives me a right to demand some faith from you; I am the same, and hope that you have not changed towards me.

Yours truly, Baratynskij

[2] Leonard Euler (1707-1783), mathematician and physicist, professor and member of the Imperial Petersburg and Berlin Academies of Sciences.
[3] "Razgovor s V. F. Bulgarinym" appeared in *Mnemozina*, 1824, Pt. 3, and was by way of a polemical continuation of the article "O napravlenii našej poèzii, osobenno liričeskoj, v poslednee desjatiletie" (*ibid.*, Pt. 2). Kjuxel'beker attacked the "half-Russian Jeremiads" who, under the influence of Žukovskij, wrote in the style of German elegiac poets of the last years of the eighteenth century. Such "mournful elegies" were also deplored by A. A. Bestužev, in "Vzgljad na staruju i novuju slovesnost' v Rossii" (1823), K. F. Ryleev (see A. G. Cejtlin, *Tvorčestvo Ryleeva*, Moscow, 1955, 237-258), and by Puškin, in "Solovej i kukuška" (1825). Baratynskij's position was curious; he, too, reproached Žukovskij for having introduced the German bards into Russia

("Bogdanoviču", 1824, 11. 25-34), yet had written numerous elegies to which, by the criteria laid down in the article praised by Baratynskij, Kjuxel'beker might well take exception. Indeed, although not mentioned by name, Baratynskij is attacked in it by implication. Baratynskij, as is plain from this letter, chose to ignore, or did not see, that implication.

15

To N. V. Putjata   (Late February-early March, 1825; Kjumen')[1]

In bustling Moscow you have not forgotten the Finnish hermit, dear Putjata, and I thank you: May you be blessed and long-lived on the earth.[2] I am sorry that you did not find Kjuxel'beker: he is an entertaining person in many respects, and sooner or later he will be remarked upon, among our writers, as an author in Rousseau's vein.[3] He has great gifts and his character greatly resembles that of the eccentric of Geneva: that same sensitivity and distrust, that same restless pride, drawing him to immoderate opinions in order to distinguish himself by an original turn of thought; and at times that same rapturous love of truth, of good and of the beautiful for which he is ready to sacrifice everything. A man at once worthy of respect and of pity, born for the love of fame (perhaps for fame, too), and for unhappiness. Thank you for your care of my infant poems:[4] you settled them all down in a decent manner. You will oblige me greatly if you will fulfil your promise and send *Woe from Wit*.[5] I do not understand why the Muscovites are angry at Griboedov and his comedy: for them the title is most comforting, and the contents gratifying. What am I to tell you about my life in Kjumen'? Memories of Gel'singfors fill its emptiness. In my memory I turn over with pleasure the few frank

---

[1] Taken from the original, preserved in the Baratynskij Archive, *CGALI*.
[2] A quotation from the Orthodox liturgy.
[3] The phrasing is not clear. A second possible reading might be: '...and sooner or later, as was Rousseau, will...' The first reading, however, seems preferable for syntactic reasons.
[4] *o moix stixotvornyx detkax*. Baratynskij gave Putjata a number of poems on his leaving Finland for Moscow in February 1825. Putjata delivered them to the editors of *Poljarnaja zvezda* (Bestužev and Ryleev), of *Severnje cvety* (Del'vig), of *Mnemozina* (Kjuxel'beker and Odoevskij), *Moskovskij telegraf* (Polevoj), and *Nevskij al'manax* (E. Alad'in). As would P. A. Pletnev, Putjata showed himself a faithful and reliable literary executor.
[5] An extract of A. S. Griboedov's comedy, *Gore ot uma*, had been published in the Petersburg almanac *Russkaja talija* in January 1825. Putjata seems to have read it, or perused the whole work in manuscript form, and described it in outline to Baratynskij.

hours passed with you and Muxanov. I remember our Alcine[6] with a sad reflection on human destiny. My friend, she, too, is unhappy;[7] she is a rose, the queen of flowers; but injured by the storm, the leaves hardly cling, and fall continually. Bossuet[8] said, pointing to the dead body of I forget which princess: Here she is, as death has made her for us. Of our queen, one might say: Here she is, as passions have made her. It is terrible! I saw her close by me, and she will never leave my memory. I joked and laughed with her; but even then a feeling of profound despondency was in my heart. Picture to yourself a splendid marble sepulchre beneath a happy, midday sky, surrounded by myrtles and lilacs – an enchanting sight, sweet-smelling air; but the sepulchre is still a sepulchre, and mingled with delight, sorrow pours into the heart: that is the feeling with which I would approach the woman even better known to you than to myself.

I have rambled, and it is not hard to ramble. Farewell, dear friend, whirl in the vortex of Moscow high society but do not forget your solitary friend, to whom your memory is very dear. You forgot to tell me your address. I will ask Muxanov to send this letter on to you. Farewell, I embrace you with all my heart.

E. Baratynskij

[6] Agrafena Fedorovna Zakrevskaja (1799-1879), wife of the Governor-General of Finland. Baratynskij felt physically attracted to Zakrevskaja late in 1824; she was summoned in spirit to become the heroine of the *poèma* "Bal", Nina. In 1824, he addressed "Kak mnogo ty v nemnogo dnej ..." to her. There is no evidence that a liaison existed between the two. Puškin, too, was not immune to her charms. His "bronze Venus", he informed P. A. Vjazemskij on September 1, 1828, was "amusing and kind"; without her, he would die of boredom in Petersburg (see A. S. Puškin, *Polnoe sobranie sočinenij*, 16 vols., vol. 14, Moscow, 1937-1949, 26).

[7] Or, unfortunate. Baratynskij dramatizes Zakrevskaja's state of depression, if such a depression there was in her in the winter of 1824-1825.

[8] Even allowing for Russian orthographical convention, Baratynskij misspells the abbé's name ("Bossjuet"). The quotation is from J-B. Bossuet's "Oraison Funèbre"on the occasion of the burial of a Duchess of Orléans (1670).

16

To N. V. Putjata   (March, 1825; Kjumen')[1]

I have received your second letter from Moscow, dear Pujata, and thank you for it. I read its opening lines with lively interest. If my comparison

[1] Taken from the original, preserved in the Baratynskij Archive, *CGALI*.

is apt, then your spreading it is touching; but the cold of the sepulchre has not yet deadened your heart completely: it is alive to friendship and to all that is good and beautiful. Delusions are inseparable from the human state, and some of them do greater honour to our hearts than a premature understanding of certain truths:

> We need both passions and dreams,
> In them is the condition and food of our existence.
> You will not subject to simple laws
> Either the world's noise or the graveyard's quiet.[2]

Why regret a strong emotion which, if it has shaken the heart profoundly, has perhaps also developed many qualities in it that have been sleeping hitherto? Will you not wish to see matters from a new viewpoint and, instead of our sepulchre, remember Shakespeare's plough, tearing up and enriching the earth?[3]

But you will never come to an end, when the question is one of comparison. Your fairy[4] has already returned to Gel'singfors. Prince L'vov accompanied her. In Fridrisgam she signed the postal book[5] as follows: Prince Chou-Chérie, heir presumptive to the kingdom of the Moon, with part of his court and one half of his seraglio.[6] A natural or convulsive gaiety never leaves her. I saw the general on his passing through F(ridris)gam. It seems that I have little hope of promotion; but so be it. Muxanov is no longer an adjutant, and the company quarters have lost

[2] The penultimate strophe of "Čerep" by the verse collection of 1835 (*Stixotvorenija Evgenija Baratynskogo: dve časti*). The strophe did not appear in the version published in *Severnye cvety* in 1825.

[3] Tim. IV, 3, 193-194(?).

[4] A. F. Zakrevskaja; see note 6 to letter 15.

[5] Travellers hiring horses would sign at changing-posts, by way of acknowledging receipt. Prince Aleksandr Dmitrievič L'vov (1800-1866) was an adjutant to Zakrevskij. Zakrevskaja, as wife of the Finnish Governor-General (the "*baba* of Abo", as he was somewhat unfairly called in the revolutionary song of the day "Car' naš nemec russkij..."), would certainly have had a government order for post-horses (*podorožnaja*). Bickering with intransigant post-masters would thus have caused Prince L'vov's blood-pressure to rise only occasionally. The rate of 'fares' for posting was, in 1824, far cheaper than in Western Europe; even in 1830, Robert Pinkerton paid no more than 5d per English mile, and this with three horses (*op. cit.*, 21). The peasants who supplied the horses would be paid (*na čaj*) according to the traveller's satisfaction. Each verst was marked on well-travelled routes (such as that from Petersburg to Vyborg) by a black-and-white pole ten feet high.

[6] The unilingual postmaster would have been unable to read the entry of the nobility. Friedriksgam, or Fridrisgam, had seen many Russian visitors since, on May 4, 1790, the Russian fleet suffered a defeat there at the hands of the Swedes, losing twenty-six ships out of sixty-three. By 1825 it was a resort.

half their charm for me. You are the only one I have left at the Gel'singfors court.[7] The others are more than strangers to me.

Won't you call on me in Kjumen'? I live in the house of the regimental commander,[8] and have my own room. You would make me very happy!

I am writing a new *poèma*.[9] Here is an extract from a description of a Moscow ball for you:

> The spacious hall gleams
> With a thousand lights; from high balconies
> Fiddlesticks drone; a crowd of guests;
> With looks of becoming importance,
> In undone, patterned bonnets,
> Sits a particoloured row of elderly
> Matrons. In their boredom, the cranks
> Now twitch their finery,
> Now, having crossed their arms, gaze
> At the crowd with dull attention.
> Young ladies swirl around,
> Their glances blazing blissfully;
> Their head-dresses sparkle
> With the fire of precious stones.
> At their half-bared shoulders
> Fly golden ringlets;
> Dresses as light as smoke
> Show off their slight figures.
> Around these captivating Graces
> Bustles and seethes
> A crowd of ardent suitors;
> They catch each glance with agitation;
> Jesting, the sorceresses make of them
> The happy and unhappy.
> All are in motion. Burning to secure
> Beauty's flattering attention,
> The cavalier twirls his moustaches,
> The civilian dandy primly casts off witticisms.[10]

---

[7]   Zakrevskij's staff headquarters was lightly referred to as 'Zakrevskij's court' by its habitués and officers.

[8]   G. A. Lutkovskij; see note 2 to letter 10.

[9]   "Bal". Baratynskij began work on the *poèma* in February 1825 and finished it only in October 1828, in Moscow. Marriage and setting up home caused lengthy delays. Extracts appeared in *Moskovskij telegraf*, 1827, Pt. 3, no. 1, and in *Severnye cvety* for 1828, before the piece was completed.

[10]   Lines 4-32. Baratynskij made many alterations to this version (as published in *Dve povesti v stixax*, 1828 – the other *povest'* being Puškin's *Graf Nulin*), before reprinting it in the collection of 1835; for this, revised version, see *1951 edition* 362 ff.

17

To N. V. Putjata   (29 March, 1825; Kjumen')[1]

I slandered you in my heart, dear Putjata; I thought you had already come to Gel'singfors, and not seen me. Your letter made me very happy. Come, come, I will embrace you with the fondest friendship.

For what reason are you awaiting letters from the general, to allow you to return to company headquarters? Is it possible that you, too, wish to leave Finland? With whom will you leave me? How many changes have come about in two months!

Thank you for your praise of my extract. You will discern impressions of Gel'singfors in the *poèma* itself. *She*[2] is my heroine. I have two hundred lines written already. Come, you can see and judge them, and I could not find a better or juster critic.

The Moscow censor[3] is either as innocent as a five-year-old girl or as gay as a drunken procuress; is it possible to allow such an indecent poem as "Leda" to be published?[4] Did Odoevskij really print my name beneath it? May God preserve me! I shall be unable to look ladies who read, in the eyes! What's one to write after that? My Leda kisses her swan publicly, but my storm is not allowed to blow.[5] Inscrutable are your ways, O Russian censorship!

There is much that is amusing in Russia; but I am not inclined to laughter; in me, joviality is the effort of a proud mind, not a child of the heart. From my very childhood I found dependence burdensome and was sullen and unhappy. In my youth fate took me into her hands. All this serves as nourishment for genius; but that's the trouble: I am not a genius. Why did it all happen thus, and not in another way? At that question, all the devils would roar with laughter.

And that answer would serve as an answer to a free-thinker; but not to me, and not to you: we believe in something. We believe in the beautiful and in virtue. Some improvement in my ability to value the good, some improvement in myself – these are treasures to be bought neither by the rich man with his money, nor by the lucky with his luck, nor by genius itself, if badly used.

Farewell, dear Putjata, I embrace you with all my heart.

Baratynskij

[1]   Taken from the original, preserved in the Baratynskij Archive, *CGALI*.
[2]   A. F. Zakrevskaja; see note 6 to letter 15.

[3] Lit. 'censorship' (*cenzura*).

[4] "Leda", a free translation of the Chevalier de Parny's poem of that title, appeared in *Mnemozina*, 1825, Pt. 4, 221. If not indecent, the poem certainly contains lines that raised eyebrows among persons of delicate sensibilities. The very water "kisses" Leda, so alluring is her body; a "childish cry" and "moan of pleasure" sum up the loss of innocence – and the discovery.

[5] "Burja" appeared in *Mnemozina*, 1825, Pt. 4, 214. In the collection of 1827 it was printed with various minor alterations. In 1835 the title and lines 10 to 20 were replaced, at the censor's request, by modest dots. Baratynskij's suspicion that the storm might not be allowed to blow itself out proved correct.

18

To I. I. Kozlov   (April, 1825; Kjumen')[1]

He is risen indeed,[2] dear and respected Ivan Ivanovič, and rumours of it reach us, but is that enough to believe? Of course, they know that better where you are, in the enlightened city,[3] than in our dark backwoods. Thank you for your kind letter, I am very glad that, by starting to write to me in Russian, you allow me to do the same. For the most part we conversed in French, and for that reason I began a correspondence with you in a language of which, not having used it for so long, I had forgotten the orthography and very phrasing. In your company I return to native soil.

Our regiment will be in Petersburg this summer. My heart leaps with joy when I think that I shall soon be in the circle of my true friends and shall embrace you, dear brother poet. Your "Venetian Night"[4] is, without flattery, delightful. In it a luxurious dreaminess blends subtly with dark rêverie. The description of Venice is filled with a special midday light;[5] and the passage in which the beauty directs her gondola towards the sea is practically the best in the whole poem. So it seems to me, and I give my opinion quite plainly because you yourself invited me to do so. I await *The Monk*[6] with impatience and thank you for your praise of the extract

[1] Taken from the *1951 edition*, 480-482.
[2] The replique to the Orthodox Russian Easter greeting ("Christ is risen! He is risen indeed").
[3] St. Petersburg.
[4] A celebrated poem by Kozlov, published in *Poljarnaja zvezda*, 1825 (March 25). It contains fine descriptive passages of Venice at night; on the machinery of moonlight, roses, Brenta and gondolas, see V. Nabokov, *Eugene Onegin*, 4 vols., vol. 1 (New York, 1964), 184-185.
[5] Lit. '...a kind of midday bliss' (or 'sweet bliss').
[6] *Černec* appeared in 1825; see *A. S. Puškin, 1962*, vol. 9, 167; *V. G. Belinskij*, vol. 3, 310-312. Baratynskij shared the prevailing enthusiasm for the *poèma*.

from "Eda".[7] I took advantage of your advice in the third part and tried to include more lyrical movement in it than in the first two.

"The Elysian Fields" was written four years ago:[8] it is a French trifle, and fit only for an almanac. I have half written a new small *poèma*. Something will come of it! The main character is ticklish,[9] but rules the piece like a bold god. Here is what they say about my heroine in Moscow:

> Whom does she entice into her house?
> Is it not inveterate gallants,
> Is it not pretty novices?
> Is not people's hearing wearied
> By the talk of her shameless victories
> And suggestive connections?

And here is what I add:

> Flee her: there is no heart in her!
> Fear the bewitching lure
> Of her insinuating speech,
> Do not catch her enamoured glances:
> In her is the ardour of the intoxicated Bacchante,
> The ardour of fever, not of love![10]

You speak of our journalists; but, praise God, we do not receive a single journal here, and no one prevents my loving poetry. I saw Polevoj only once before his departure for Moscow: he seemed to me an enthusiast not unlike Kjuxel'beker.[11] If he raves, he raves with a good heart, and at least he is conscientious. Vjazemskij[12] is most annoying of all. He was educated in the troubled times of Karamzin's wars with Šiškov,[13] and even now the martial spirit has not left him:

> By journalistic war he dishonours without reason
>   His gifts:
> Was it not thus that Catherine's friend, the famous captain
>   Orlov yet loved fist fights?[14]

This is impromptu; and I think that, as verse, it is outstanding. Farewell.

Yours truly, Baratynskij

[7]   An extract from "Eda" was published in *Poljarnaja zvezda* for 1825. Within a few months of this letter, further extracts had been printed in *Mnemozina*, 1825, Pt. 4 and in *Moskovskij telegraf*, 1825, no. 22.

[8]   It was not published, however, until 1825 (*Poljarnaja zvezda*, 103).

[9]   Arsenij, hero of "Bal".

[10]   Lines 65-70, 107-112 by the 1835 version.

[11]   V. K. Kjuxel'beker was indeed an enthusiast, as his celebrated Parisian speech made clear (October 1820). He was punished for that enthusiasm by Nicholas's *gendarmerie*; see B. Mejlax, "Vil'gel'm Kjuxel'beker" in *Stixotvorenija V. K. Kjuxel'-bekera* (Leningrad, 1952), and V. G. Bazanov, "Vil'gel'm Kjuxel'beker", *Očerki dekabristskoj literatury: poèzija* (Moscow, 1961).

[12]   Baratynskij made the acquaintance on leaving Finland and settling in Moscow, in 1825. He was already, of course, acquainted with Vjazemskij's verse and criticism.

[13]   The allusion is to the lengthy polemics – a matter of history by 1825 – between 'the Karamzinists' and supporters of Admiral A. S. Šiškov in the last decade of the eighteenth century and first years of the nineteenth. Šiškov opposed Karamzin's new, Gallicized Russian, favouring a return to the "genuine, Old Slavonic tongue". On the dispute, see A. Martel, *Michel Lomonosov et La Langue Littéraire Russe* (Paris, 1933).

[14]   The epigram was not published until 1899, in *Ostaf'evskij arxiv*, vol. 3, 119. Commercial literature and professional critics moved Baratynskij to unusual heights of irony; see letter 12 and "Bogdanoviču" (1824), 11.59-68. It is ironical, too, that Baratynskij should have been nominated literary critic on Kireevskij's *Evropeec* (see letter 39), and that his own review of A. N. Murav'ev's "Tavrida" (*1951 edition*, 421-425), should so admirably exemplify the clarity of exposition that he demands in that same article.

19

To A. I. Turgenev   (9 May, 1825; Kjumen')[1]

Your Excellency, Gracious Sir, Aleksandr Ivanovič!

At last I am free,[2] and I am indebted to you for my freedom. Your magnanimous, persistent petitioning has returned me to society, to my family, to life! Your Excellency, accept a poor recompense for the great service that you have done me, accept a few words of gratitude, unnecessary to you, perhaps, but necessary to my heart. Already for several days everything around me has breathed gaiety: my good comrades congratulate me from their hearts, and their felicitations belong to you! Soon I shall return to my family, there tears of joy will flow, and it will be you who extorts them! May God and your heart reward you.[3]

With true respect and perfect devotion I have the honour to remain, Gracious Sir, your Excellency's most humble servant,

Evgenij Baratynskij

[1]   Taken from the *1951 edition*, 482.

[2]   The decree by which Baratynskij was promoted officer was signed by Alexander in Warsaw on April 21, 1825. Baratynskij well appreciated the extent of his indebtedness to A. I. Turgenev, beside whose persistent campaigning in the poet's cause even the

contributions of Zakrevskij and Žukovskij paled. It was Žukovskij, however, who first interested Turgenev in the exile's case.

³ The sentimental appeal of this paragraph, nicely calculated by its author, recalls that of the verse (and letters) of Turgenev himself, twenty years earlier; see M. Ehrhard, *op. cit.*, 50-62. At the conclusion of this letter, in the left-hand corner, are written the words: "Kjumen' gorod. Maja 9 dnja 1825".

20

To N. V. Putjata   (Early August, 1825; Petersb)[1]

I am to blame, dear Putjata, I am to blame, but not for my heart, which is truly devoted to you, but for my careless and lazy disposition. I have not written to you for a long time, but have not stopped thinking of you, nor have I ceased to remember our life in Gel'singfors and your friendly visit to Kjumen'.[2]

You can imagine how the unexpected meeting with Agr(afena) Fed-(orovna),[3] with Misin'ka[4] and, finally, with Karolina Levander,[5] who had almost completely left my memory, amazed and delighted me. I have already seen them twice. Agrafena Fedorovna treats me very kindly, and although I know it is dangerous even to glance at her, I seek and desire that tormenting pleasure. I am thinking of being in Gel'singfors in September, to thank the General for my resurrection and to be with you.

I am leaving many details until the next post. Agrafena Fedorovna will give you this letter. Very kindly she volunteered to do so. And she can explain to you why I did not manage to write to you, why I did not come to Pargolovo and so on and so forth.

I accompanied Muxanov to Moscow: he left restless and melancholy, and will always remain so. What an unhappy gift is an intellect that too easily[6] overwhelms the imagination! What an unhappy fruit of premature experience is a heart hungry for happiness but already incapable of surrendering itself to one constant passion and losing itself in a mass of

---

¹ Taken from the original, preserved in the Baratynskij Archive, *CGALI*.
² In early May, 1825, N. V. Putjata came to Kjumen' with the news of Baratynskij's promotion.
³ Zakrevskaja; see note 6 to letter 15.
⁴ An English governess of the Zakrevskijs.
⁵ Karolina Levander spoke English, and may conceivably have been of English parentage; she had lived all her life in Finland, however, and was in 1825 a companion to A. F. Zakrevskaja.
⁶ Lit. 'imagination, by too much exceeded by reason'.

limitless desires! Such is Muxanov's situation, and mine, and that of most young people of our time.[7]

We are returning to Finland in a few days, and I am almost glad: senseless dissipation[8] has wearied me, I need to withdraw into myself; having withdrawn, I shall certainly meet you, and shall write to you more often. You will see from the form of this letter, I think, in what disorder my thoughts are. Farewell, dear Putjata, until I have leisure, until I have common sense and, of course, until we meet. I am hurrying to her:[9] you will suspect that I am a little infatuated. A little, yes; but I hope that my first hours of solitude will return my reason to me. I shall write a few elegies and fall asleep peacefully. Poetry is a wonderful charm: casting its own spell, it renders powerless all other harmful spells. Farewell, I embrace you.

Baratynskij

I first thought of giving the enclosed letter to Magdalina[10] to deliver; but it seemed to me that I had put dangerous details in it. I am sending this by post, and will give her, in a sealed envelope, a sheet of plain paper. How her curiosity will be punished, should she unseal my letter! Farewell.

[7] The situation of Adolphe and, in different terms, of a whole generation who came to maturity in time to see all hope of liberal action destroyed in one rising.
[8] The suggestion is that time has been wasted, or futilely employed.
[9] To A. F. Zakrevskaja; see note 6 to letter 15.
[10] A. F. Zakrevskaja.

21

To A. S. Puškin[1]   (Early December, 1825; Moscow)[2]

Thank you for your letter, dear Puškin: it made me very happy, for I

[1] There is a considerable volume of scholarship on the relationship between Puškin and Baratynskij. For a bibliography, see *Muratova*, 140. Each highly respected the work of the other, and Puškin regarded Baratynskij as the first and greatest Russian elegiac poet; see *A. S. Puškin, 1962*, vol. 6, 369-372. He also praised Baratynskij's album pieces (*Evgenij Onegin*, 3), epigrams and erotica (*A. S. Puškin, 1962*, vol. 9, 37). The elegy "Priznanie" he thought "a wonder" (*ibid.*, vol. 9, 88). Puškin's admiration for Baratynskij the poet mingled with his admiration for Baratynskij the man. Baratynskij, for his part, fully appreciated Puškin's personal genius and, not unnaturally, was "over shadowed, so to speak, weighed down" by it; see *P. A. Vjazemskij, 1883*, vol. 7, 268-269. The two shared a common social, cultural and literary background, yet their outlooks were totally at variance. Baratynskij was a determinist and pessimist in the mould of a Leopardi. The difference in outlook served only to strengthen mutual respect.

prize your memory greatly.[3] The attention that you give my rhymed trifles would make me think a great deal of their worth, did I not know that you are as kind in your letters as you are exalted and moving in your poetical works.[4]

Do not think that I am so much the marquis[5] that I cannot feel the beauty[6] of a romantic tragedy! I love Shakespeare's heroes, almost always natural, always entertaining, in the true dress of their times and with strongly drawn characters.[7] I prefer them to the heroes of Racine, but do justice to the French tragedian's great talent. I will say more: I am almost convinced that the French can have no true romantic tragedy. It is not the rules of Aristotle that lay fetters on them – it is easy to free oneself of those –, but they are without the most important means to success: an elegant popular speech.[8] I respect the French classics, they knew their language and occupied themselves with those forms of poetry natural to them, producing much that is beautiful. I find their latest romantics pitiful: it seems to me that they have sat in someone else's sled.

I am panting to have an idea of your Godunov. Our wonderful language is suited for any purpose; I feel this, though I cannot bring it to realization. It was made for Puškin, and Puškin for it. I am certain that your tragedy is filled with exceptional qualities. Go, complete what has been begun, you, in whom genius has settled! Raise Russian poetry to that eminence among the poetry of all peoples to which Peter the Great raised Russia among the powers. Accomplish alone what he accomplished alone; our part is gratitude and wonder.[9]

Vjazemskij is not in Moscow; but I shall visit him at Ostaf'evo[10] in a

---

[2] This letter is taken from A. S. Puškin, *Polnoe sobranie sočinenij*, 16 vols., vol. 13 (Moscow, 1937-1949), 253, checked against the original in *Puškinskij Dom*, F. 244, op. 2, no. 9.

[3] Baratynskij was introduced to Puškin by Del'vig in the late summer or autumn of 1818, See V. Gaevskij, "A. A. Del'vig", *Sovremennik*, vol. 39 (1853), no. 5, 35-48.

[4] A just comment. Puškin was liberal of his praise for the work of his contemporaries, among whom there were few, as V. Brjusov pointed out (*Izbrannye sočinenija*, 2 vols., vol. 2, Moscow, 1955, 461-462), of whom he did not make some comment.

[5] *Le marquis* — Baratynskij's *soubriquet* among his Petersburg friends and acquaintances in 1818-1824; the influence of such neo-classical poets as Chénier, Millevoye, Gabriel Legouvé and Parny was, indeed, considerable on his earliest verse; see my paper, "18th-century Neo-classical French influences on Puškin and E. A. Baratynskij", *Comparative Literature Studies*, vol 6 (1969), no. 4, 435-461.

[6] Lit. 'the beauties...'

[7] Lit. '...faces'.

[8] Lit. 'simple-popular', or 'of the common people' (*prostonarodnogo*).

[9] See the introductory comments to this letter.

[10] The Vjazemskij estate near Moscow.

day or two and will carry out your commission. I have read Kjuxel'beker's Spirits.[11] Not bad, but not good either. His gaiety is not gay, and the poetry is weak and tongue-tied. I am not copying "Eda" for you because it will be off the press within a day or two. Del'vig, who is looking after the edition in P(etersbur)g, will immediately send you one copy, very likely two, if you will not shirk doing for me what you did for Ryleev.[12] I very much want to visit you: but God knows when I shall manage to do so. I shall certainly not let an opportunity slip by. Meanwhile we will exchange letters. Write, dear Puškin, and I will not remain in your debt, although I write to you with that constraint with which one usually writes to elders.

Farewell, I embrace you. Why do you call Levuška Lev Sergeevič?[13] He loves you sincerely, and if he has somehow disgraced himself in your eyes through his frivolity, it is your part to be indulgent. I know that you have long been angry with him; but it is not good to be angry for a long time. I am meddling in others' business, but you will forgive me for it, remembering my affection for you and for your brother.

Yours truly, Baratynskij

My address: in Moscow, by Xariton in the Ogorodniki, Mjasoedova's house.

[11] *Šekspirovy duxi* (1825), a light dramatic piece.
[12] Puškin wrote comments on the edges of many pages of the separate edition of Ryleev's *Vojnarovskij* (1824-1825).
[13] Lev Puškin's indiscretions were numerous and infamous. Not only was he negligent in money matters; he circulated his brother's MS poems, reciting them at parties and allowing admirers to transcribe them.

22

To A. S. Puškin   (5-20 January, 1826; Moscow)[1]

I am sending you *Uranija*,[2] dear Puškin; the treasure is not great; but blessed is he who is satisfied with little. We need philosophy urgently.

[1] Taken from A. S. Puškin, *Polnoe sobranie sočinenij*, vol. 13 (Moscow, 1937-1949), 25 and checked with *1884 edition*, 504.
[2] *Uranija*, a journal edited by M. P. Pogodin, had a life-span of nine months in 1826. Baratynskij placed two poems in it — "K — pri posylke tetradi stixov" and "Ožidanie". The former appeared in the *1884 edition* with the heading: "G.Z." (Grafine Zakrevskoj), a guess, but probably an accurate one, by the editor of the Kazan' edition.

However, let me draw your attention to the piece under the title "Ja esm'".[3] The author is an eighteen-year-old boy,[4] and seems to hold promise. The style is not always precise, but there is poetry, especially in the beginning. At the end it is metaphysics, too abstruse for verse. I must tell you that Muscovite youth is possessed by transcendental philosophy.[5] I do not know if this is good or bad; I have not read Kant and admit that I do not understand the latest aesthetes too well. Galič has produced a poetic[6] in the German manner. Platonic notions are revived in it and brought into a system, with a few additions. Not knowing German, I was delighted at the opportunity to become acquainted with German aesthetics. It has its own particular poetry which is pleasing, but, it seems to me, its premises might be refuted philosophically. How is this your concern, however, especially yours? Create what is beautiful, and let others break their heads over it. How you trimmed the elegiacs in your epigram![7] It caught me too, and serves me right; it occurred to me before you, and in one unpublished poem I say that

The mincing cries of the poets of our times
                                        have become very sham.[8]

They write to tell me that you are starting on[9] a new *poèma* on Ermak. The subject is truly poetic, and worthy of you. They say that even Camoens[10] goggled when the news reached Parnassus. May God bless you and strengthen your muscles for the mighty deed.

I often see Vjazemskij. The other day we read your short poems together, thinking to run over a few pieces but reading through the whole book.[11] What do you plan to do with Godunov? Are you printing it, or trying it first on the stage? I am dying to read it. Farewell, dear Puškin, do not forget me.

E. Baratynskij

---

[3]   A poem by S. P. Ševyrev (1806-1864), soon to attack Baratynskij's verse collection in sharply hostile terms (see *1936 edition*, vol. 1, LXXX-LXXXII) and to remain a critic of Baratynskij's work until the latter's death. Ševyrev would see "shades of the earlier elegiac poet" in the author of "Osen'" (1837) (!), writing in *Moskovskij nabljuda-tel'*, 1837, Pt. 12, 319-324. Ševyrev, whose most successful piece was perhaps "Son" (a remarkable outpouring of 53 iambic tetrameters, 1827), was a skilled but cantankerous critic. He specialized in archaic, myth-laden imagery, of which "Ja esm'" is far from bare.
[4]   Baratynskij was mistaken; in the spring of 1826, Ševyrev was approaching 21.
[5]   The allusion is to the 'Lovers of Wisdom' (*Ljubomudry*), whom Baratynskij came to meet through Puškin's good offices. (On October 24, 1826, the two attended a dinner in Moscow given to celebrate the founding of the Germanophile journal *Moskovskij vestnik*; see *Puškin i ego sovremenniki*, Pts. 19-20, 80.) V. F. Odoevskij, Ševyrev,

Venevitinov, Pogodin and Kjuxel'beker were also known as "the archive youths" (*Evgenij Onegin*, 7, 49), a name seemingly coined for those half-hearted employees of the Office of Records at the Foreign Office by Sergej Sobolevskij; so, at least, Puškin claims in a draft for a critical article; Lenin Library, 2387A, f.22ʳ. Of all civil institutions, only the Foreign Office was quite the thing for young noblemen in the mid-1820s; and only the Office of Records happened to be in Moscow. Puškin's motives for introducing Baratynskij to the group, in whose work, Puškin knew, Baratynskij's participation could never be more than marginal, were not disinterested. It was possible, Puškin informed Vjazemskij (*A. S. Puškin, 1962*, vol. 9, 244), that he and not Pogodin would shortly be the proprietor of *Moskovskij vestnik*. This was within nine months of Baratynskij's writing the present letter. The matter depended on the moral and financial support that he succeeded in raising. With that end in mind, Puškin wrote to V. Tumanskij (*ibid.*, 254), as well as to Vjazemskij, Jazykov, Baratynskij and others; but from a letter to Pogodin himself of August-September, 1827 (*ibid.*, 263) it is plain that he did not succeed in his attempt. But he watched over Pogodin, ready to criticize (*ibid.*, 273), and Baratynskij, willy-nilly, was involved.

⁶ By *poètika*, Baratynskij seems to mean 'aesthetic treatise'. Aleksandr Ivanovič Galič (1783-1848), first Professor of Philosophy at St. Petersburg University (1819), was a committed Schellingian. The work referred to is his *Opyt nauki izjaščnogo* (1825), published separately, also in 1825, by I. Smirdin. Galič drew extensively on the works of such German theorists of art as Schelling and Friedrich Bouterwek (1766-1828).

⁷ "Solovej i kukuška" (1825).

⁸ The line was never printed; in an altered form, it appeared in "Podražateljam", (11.7-8), published only in 1830 (*Moskovskij vestnik*, Pt. 1, no. 1, 7).

⁹ Lit. 'you are venturing/undertaking...'

¹⁰ Luis Camoens (1525-1580), Portuguese poet, author of the Panoramic "Lusiada".

¹¹ Puškin's first book of verse appeared only in 1826.

23

To N. V. Putjata.   (16-22 January, 1826; Moscow)¹

Thank you for your letters, dear Putjata. One of them brought a double benefit: it gave me great pleasure and it calmed your mother, who had no news of you for some time and was a little distressed.²

It is no wonder that the description of Finland³ that you found in *The*

¹ Taken from *Russkij Arxiv*, 1867, bk. 2, 273-274. Dated by the postmark.

² Ekaterina Ivanovna Putjata, née Efimoviča (?-1833).

³ An extract from the opening strophes of "Eda". "Eda" was written in Finland, completed and reworked in Moscow in the following year (1825). Wild storms in the Gulf of Finland in November 1824 inspired Baratynskij's "Burja", as well as Puškin's "Mednyj vsadnik". In the 1820s, it was visited by occasional sight-seers; by 1840 the trickle had become a steady flow; see Ja. K. Grot, "O Finljandii", *Sovremennik*, vol. 18 (1840), 5-82. The extent of the increase of interest in the delightfully Ossianic Grand Duchy may be judged by P. A .Pletnev's decision to publish, in 1842, an almanac commemorating the two-hundredth anniversary of the founding of Helsinki University (The Imperial Alexandrine University of Gel'singfors). The almanac was called *Finljandija v russkoj poèzii*; its content may be found in *Sočinenija i perepiska P. A. Pletneva*, 3 vols., vol. 1 (St.P., 1883), 445-455.

Telegraph[4] had escaped your notice. It was written not in Gel'singfors but in Moscow. In a day or two my "Eda" will be coming out,[5] and I will send you a copy immediately. I thank the amiable Butkov,[6] F. V. Bulgarin's fond admirer, for his comment; but I will add my word. In poetry one writes not what is, but what seems to be. On the edge of the horizon cliffs touch the sky, consequently "rise up to" the sky. In prose I am guilty, but in poetry almost right. Meanwhile, here is a little epistle to Butkov's friend for his amusement:

> In your sheets you meanly play the hypocrite,
> You disfigure both opinions and stories;
> In a friendly way you flatter buffoonery,
> Talent you enviously defame;
> Your ugly disposition bears its ugly fruit:
> Shameless, shameless! everyone whispers. – That's the news!
> But don't grieve, I'm just settling an account:
> *My* dishonour's paid for by subscribers.[7]

I am thinking of sending a well-bound copy of "Eda" to the General. I forgot to wish him a prosperous new year; and now it is too late. I am very embarrassed about this. I would not wish him to think that I have forgotten my benefactor. Good-for-nothing poet's unconcern!

I am bored in Moscow. New acquaintances are unbearable to me. My heart demands friendship, not civilities, and a well-bred putting on of airs inspires a heavy feeling in me. I look on the people around me with cold irony. I return greetings with greetings, and suffer.

Often I think of tried friends, of the earlier comrades of my life – all are far away! And when shall we meet? Moscow is a new exile for me. Why do we grieve in a foreign land? There, no one speaks about our past life. Is not Moscow that same foreign land for me? Forgive me my faint-heartedness, but in wearisome Finland you will learn, perhaps with some pleasure, that even in Moscow good people are wearied. Farewell, my dear friend, I embrace you. I thank Alexander[8] for not forgetting me; I remember him and you very well.

Baratynskij

[4] *Moskovskij telegraf*, 1825, no. 22, 157.
[5] *Eda, Finljandskaja povest', i Piry, opisatel'naja poèma* (St.P., 1826); censor's permission as of November 2, 1825; 56 pp. The *poèma* appeared without the epilogue written for it; it was sent to Kjuxel'beker via Putjata in February 1825, but banned by the censor (see "Pis'mo N. V. Putjata k A. A. Muxanovu", *Russkij arxiv*, 1905, no. 3, 524; letter of March 9, 1825). It was then sent to Bestužev and Ryleev for inclusion in the radical *Poljarnaja zvezda*, where it also failed to appear.
[6] Petr Grigor'evič Butkov (1775-1857), civil servant and historian.

⁷ The epigram was not published until 1884 (*1884 edition*, 527).
⁸ Probably Putjata's younger brother, then serving in the 46th Chasseurs.

24

To M. E. Lobanov   (1826; Moscow)[1]

My fate is such, respected Mixail Evstaf'evič, that I never can say before-hand if I will do a thing or not. Not everyone has moved yet, but you have perhaps already heard from Del'vig that I have changed my place of residence, and together with it my circumstances, too, have changed. I am most ashamed that I cannot keep my word, but must decisively decline work for which I have no leisure – and for which, besides, I feel myself unfitted. Scold me: I deserve it. But do not change in your[2] good opinion of me, which I, too, deserve in some measure, valuing it very highly.

Yours truly, E. Baratynskij

[1] Taken from the original, preserved in Puškinskij Dom, under reference: R. 1, op. 2, no. 214 (Baratynskij, E. A.). It is described as follows: "Pis'mo E. A. Baratynskogo k Lobanovu, M.E. Iz al'boma Ponomarevoj". It is on a single sheet, written in poor script.

Mixail Evstaf'evič Lobanov (1787-1846) was of an older generation than Baratynskij. He served in the St. Petersburg Public Library, where he came to know Del'vig — also working under I. Krylov. He was a writer, translator and critic, and distinguished in no one field. Among his works were "Oda rossijskomu vojstvu" (1813), "Pesn' na vzjatie Pariža" (1816) and the weak translations "Ifegenija v Alvide" (1816) and "Fedra" (1823). Within a year of Puškin's *Boris Godunov*, his own version had appeared, ponderously 'classical' and without Puškin's interludes of humour. It was a failure.

Since Baratynskij refers to Del'vig, the letter cannot date from later than January 1831. A "change of place of residence" occurred in 1825-1826, when Baratynskij moved to Moscow — where Lobanov lived.

The letter in which Lobanov asked the poet to collaborate on an unknown work has not survived. Having earlier agreed to such a project, Baratynskij now plainly finds that he has neither time nor interest to spare. He had "no leisure" in 1826 because of his marriage (on June 9), because of his preparation of proof-copies for the 1827 collection of his verse, and because of the urgency of his domestic re-arrangements.

Baratynskij excuses himself gracefully, insinuating that Lobanov's good opinion is of great moment to him (of which there is no evidence elsewhere), and declines to help the *klassik*. The fact of Baratynskij's acquaintance with Lobanov suggests that he had a wide range of connections in the literary world, in all parties and groups.

[2] Indistinctly written.

25

To N. A. Polevoj.   (25 November, 1827; Mara)[1]

Dear Nikolaj Alekseevič, I have received "Diva"[2], "Onegin"[3] and my verses. It seems to me that you reviewed "Diva" fairly in *The Telegraph*. Podolinskij[4] has talent, of course. What can one say about "Onegin"? What a wonder! What a brilliant style, appropriate and free! It is the sketch of a Raphaël, the live, unconstrained brush of an artist among artists. Concerning myself, I cannot say how much I am indebted to you. The edition is delightful.[5] Without you, I would never have succeeded in appearing in print in such splendid fashion. I am very, very grateful. Complete your kindness by fulfilling one more most humble request. Send 600 copies to Baron Anton Antonovič Del'vig. On great Millionnaja, in the house of Mme Ebeling. We have our private reckonings and accounts. Do not refuse to distribute the remainder according to your discretion. Money, of course, is needed for the dispatch of such a number of copies; perhaps you do not have any ready money, and I am therefore writing to my father-in-law[6] and asking him to give you 100. Even without this, I am much indebted to you. Allow me to assure you that if the edition does not pay for itself I shall all the same be a reliable debtor. Be so kind, on the release of the edition, to furnish my father-in-law with 12 copies, including one on Alexandrine paper. They are for distribution among my Moscow relatives. I would also ask you, dear Nikolaj Alekseevič, to send one copy each to P(rince) Vjazemskij, Dmitriev,[7] and Pogodin; ask your young brother to accept my trifles as keepsakes of me, and honour your own personal copy[8] by placing it in your library between Batjuškov and V. L. Puškin.[9] Send me a further 8 copies. How many commissions! It is hard to be involved with a poet. Forgive me all this in the name of Phoebus, esq.

Farewell, I embrace you with all my heart.

E. Baratynskij

[1]   Taken from *Russkij arxiv* (1872), bk. 2, 351-352. Nikolaj Alekseevič Polevoj (1796-1846) was of Siberian merchant stock, and an acute entrepreneur and literary journalist. His *Moskovskij telegraf*, the platform of those little in sympathy with German aesthetics and romantic writing, was commercially successful — an unusual state of affairs among literary periodicals and almanacs of the period. Polevoj was a fervent admirer of Byron, de Vigny, Balzac and Sue. He gave credit, however, to Goethe and Schiller, fragments of whose work appeared in his journal in 1825, Pt. 2; 1828, Pt. 19; 1829, Pt. 25. It was *Cinq Mars*, *Hérnani* and *Lucrécia Borgia*, however, that fired his deepest enthusiasm ("Inostrannaja literatura v 1833 godu", 1833, Pt. 49).

[2] A misspelling of one half of the title of Andrej Ivanovič Podolinskij's (1806-1886) "Div i Peri".

[3] Chapter 3, which appeared in a separate edition in October, 1827.

[4] Baratynskij is generous. Puškin correctly estimates Podolinskij's brilliant and facile verse (often no more than an imitation of his own work) as second-rate; see *A. S. Puškin, 1962*, vol. 10, 28.

[5] *Stixotvorenija Evgenija Baratynskogo* (Moscow, 1827); censor's permission as of March 28, 1827; 178 pp. *in octo*. The edition was sold, in Moscow, only in the offices of (Polevoj's) *Moskovskij telegraf.* His interest in the edition is apparent.

[6] Lev Nikolaevič Èngel'gardt (1766-1836), retired General-Major, landowner in Kazan', Muscovite.

[7] Ivan Ivanovič Dmitriev (1760-1837) was, in 1827, a revered elder. He was the author of innumerable sentimental poems, and essentially a Karamzinist.

[8] *krepostnoj èkzempljar.*

[9] Lev Sergeevič Puškin (1805-1852); see note 13 to letter 21. This letter is an interesting indication of the cordiality that existed between Polevoj and Baratynskij in the winter of 1827-1828. Within two years that friendship would sour. There is little but censure in Polevoj's review of "Naložnica", *Moskovskij telegraf*, 1831, Pt. 38, 235-243, and a total absence of correspondence suggests strongly that personal friendship was not able to survive the critical onslaught. Baratynskij's verse contained insufficient "passion", "colour" and "movement"; his last *poèma* centred on walks in boulevards and dull masked balls (!); it did not follow "the new direction" as marked out by Balzac.

26

To A. S. Puškin   (Late February-early March, 1828; Moscow)[1]

I would long ago have written to you, dear Puškin, had I known your address and had the simplest of ideas, to write to Puškin in Petersburg, not come to me late. I would probably have done that, were it not that Vjazemskij, who is leaving, has given me an opportunity to write to you – and to be sure of reaching you. In my Tambov isolation I have been very concerned about you. The rumour went about here that they had taken you away, and, as you are a rather arrestable person, I believed it. Some time later I was overjoyed to hear that *you* did some abducting, but that you were not abducted. I am now an orphan in Moscow. At least I feel your absence acutely. Del'vig stayed with me a short while. He spoke to me a lot about you: among other things, he reported one phrase of yours that saddened me a little. You told him: "Baratynskij and I do not correspond now, or I would have informed him...," and so on. Is it possible, Puškin, that since having come to know each other in Moscow

[1] Taken from A. S. Puškin, *Polnoe sobranie sočinenij*, 16 vols., vol. 14 (Moscow, 1937-1949), 5-6, and checked against M. L. Gofman's *Puškin i ego sovremenniki*, bk. 16 (St.P., 1913), 147-148.

better than before, we have drawn further apart?[2] I, at least, love the man in you and the poet as before.

Two more cantos of "Onegin" have come out here.[3] Everyone interprets them in his own way: some praise, others abuse, but they all read them. I like the broad plan of your "Onegin" very much, but the majority do not understand it. They seek a romantic plot, they seek the usual, and, of course, do not find it. The great poetic simplicity of your work seems to them poverty of imagination, they do not notice that old and new Russia, life in all its variations, passes before their eyes, but the devil take them and God bless them![4] I think that here in Russia a poet can hope for great success only with his first, immature efforts. Behind him stand all young people, finding in him almost their own feelings, almost their own thoughts, clothed in dazzling colours.[5] The poet develops, writes with greater deliberation, greater profundity; he bores the officers, but brigadiers cannot be reconciled with him because his verses, after all, are not prose. Do not take these reflections as personal: they are general. Your portrait in *Northern Flowers* is an excellent likeness[6] and is beautifully engraved. Del'vig gave me a special reprint. It now hangs in my study, in a becoming frame.[7] Vasilij L'vovič[8] is writing a romantic *poèma*. Ask Vjazemskij about it. It is a work wholly in the manner of a ballad. I picture Vasilij L'vovič to myself as a Parnassian Gromoboj,[9] who has sold his soul to the romantic devil. Is it not possible to parody Žukovskij's ballad? Meanwhile, farewell, dear Puškin! Please think kindly of me.

[2] Baratynskij and Puškin met in Moscow in the autumn and winter of 1826 and early weeks of 1827. Relations between the two continued to be warm, although they seldom met thereafter; on meeting Puškin by chance in a Kazan' hotel on the night of September 5, 1833, Baratynskij passed hours with him in animated conversation. On September 7 he brought Puškin to Kajmary, the Èngel'gardts' estate near Kazan', and entertained him there; V. A. Klimentovskij, *Russkie pisateli v Tatarskoj ASSR* (Kazan', 1951), 50-52.

[3] Chapters 4 and 5 appeared in late January and early February 1828. Chapter 4 was written in two bursts between October 1824 and the first week of 1826 (numerous works, including *Boris Godunov*, intervening). Chapter 5 was started on January 4, 1826, and completed, after the trip to Moscow and a vital conversation with the new tsar, in mid-November of that year. Baratynskij certainly knew them before they made their way to the provinces.

[4] Such French intermissions, unexpected in the Russian flow of Baratynskij's letters, are some indication that, while he naturally thought in Russian, Baratynskij could still, in 1828, happen upon a Gallic turn of phrase that expressed his thought more nicely than the equivalent Russian phrase — which eluded him.

[5] Or 'fitted in resplendent colours'.

[6] Puškin's portrait, engraved by N. Utkin from the original of O. Kiprenskij, was published in an appendix to *Severnye cvety* for 1828. Baratynskij's 'special reprint' may be seen in the *Muzej-usad'ba imeni F. I. Tjutčeva* — Muranovo — four miles' walk

NW. from the Akušinskaja railway station, 35 minutes from the Jaroslavl' Station, Moscow.

[7] *Oklady* are usually found around icons. The irony is intentional. But Baratynskij did not worship Puškin — he merely respected him deeply.

[8] Vasilij L'vovič Puškin (1767-1830) was regarded by his nephew's generation as an old man long before he was fifty. He was, however, a poet of Karamzin's age, although still quite capable in 1811 of producing such a salacious and witty poem — *galant* rather than obscene — as *Opasnyj sosed*. Puškin congratulated his uncle on the piece in *Gorodok*, Baratynskij, more obliquely, in his epigram "Otkuda vzjal Vasilij nepotešnyj...", written in December 1826.

[9] The eponymous hero of Žukovskij's ballad.

27

To N. V. Putjata   (April, 1828; Moscow)[1]

I am mortally guilty before you, my dear Putjata: I am answering your letter after three centuries; but better late than never. Do not think, however, that I do not have a grateful heart: your friendship is dear and precious to me, but what can you do about natural unpunctuality?[2]

> Forgive me, dear friend, thus the divine
> Power created me:
> I love to postpone to the morrow
> What should be done today![3]

I am not suited for any chancery, although I recently entered the Chancery of Furs;[4] but praise God, I have little to do; otherwise things would be bad for my chief.

Thank you for your friendly criticism. Your observations are just in the particular; but if we were together I would convince you, perhaps, that certain of my alterations are good for the whole. However, I by no means

[1] Taken from *Russkij arxiv* (1867), bk. 2, 277-278. Dated on the basis of Zakrevskij's appointment as Minister of Internal Affairs in April 1828.

[2] Or, inaccuracy, carelessness.

[3] First published, in this form, in *1884 edition*, 531.

[4] Baratynskij entered the government service on January 24, 1828, and worked in the chancery mentioned, in a desultory fashion, until July 1831; see *Academy edition*, vol. 1, LXVIII. His position was then filled by N. M. Jazykov; see K. K. Buxmejer, 'N. M. Jazykov', N. M. Jazykov, *Polnoe sobranie stixotvorenij* (Moscow, 1964), 42.

At what salary Baratynskij was appointed is not fully clear from the existing records. When Puškin was officially given a position with the Collegium of Foreign Affairs, in November 1831 (although he received a few roubles only in the following July), it was at 5000 roubles a year. Baratynskij's salary, three years earlier, would have been comparable.

vouch for the justness of my opinion. Poets are for the most part poor judges of their own work. The reason for this is the exceedingly complex relationship between them and their works. The pride of the intellect and the rights of the heart are in ceaseless conflict. One piece you love because you remember the feeling with which you wrote it. You are proud of a correction because you conquered an emotional feeling with the mind.[5] Which are you to trust? I am dissatisfied with one thing in your letter: it is not entirely friendly. You write to me as though to an outsider whom you fear to bore; you speak a great deal about me and not a word about yourself. How is your Alcine?[6] Does she hold you captive as before? By the way, I have heard that A(rsenij) A(ndreevič) has been made Minister of Internal Affairs; will you remain with him? Are you thinking of living in Moscow the fair? I am now a permanent resident of Moscow. I live quietly, peaceably, content with my family life, but I admit that Moscow is not to my liking. Imagine, I have not one comrade, not one person to whom I might say: Do you remember? – with whom I could open up. And that is hard. I wait for you as I wait for the rain in May. Here the atmosphere is dry, and unbelievably dusty.[7] Married people have a greater need of friendship than the single. Playing the gallant affords some small amusement to an unattached young man almost everywhere; he beats the air and mills the wind with some shapely fool and little harm comes to him. But a family man is no longer capable of that childish diversion; he needs a better diet, he needs a good companion, his equal in mind and heart, likable in himself and not because of the petty relations of a petty self-esteem. Come to see us, my dear Putjata, you will give me moments of true happiness. Farewell, forgive my laziness and other shortcomings generously. Love me because I sincerely love you. Your

Baratynskij

My address: On Nikitskaja, parish of Maloe Voznesenie, Èngel'gardt's house.
I will send a copy to Magdalina,[8] but isn't it late? Did Del'vig give you a copy from me?

---

[5] A revealing statement, seen in the perspective of Baratynskij's own verse. It was precisely his object to overcome what is (emotionally) unpleasant, and to express the true horror of human life and destiny; see "Osen'" (1837) or "Mudrecu" (1840).
[6] A. F. Zakrevskaja.
[7] Baratynskij always thought of Moscow as a dusty spot; Lermontov seemed to him, in 1839, to carry the Muscovite atmosphere with him; see *Academy edition*, vol. 1, 303.
[8] A. F. Zakrevskaja.

28

To P. A. Vjazemskij   (May, 1829; Moscow)[1]

Vasilij L'vovič has given me your present – a copy of "The Station".[2] I offer you my sincerest gratitude for this token that you have not forgotten me. You promised to busy yourself with a complete edition of your works; do not put it off: it will bring you benefit in every possible sense, and we shall have something to read and talk about. Puškin has left for Georgia.[3] When I received your letter, in which you ask for his "Poltava",[4] he was no longer in Moscow. "Poltava" is generally less well liked than Puškin's other *poèmy*. It is criticized quite without discernment. Strange! I say this not because I respect the judgement of the public overmuch and am amazed that on this occasion it is wrong; but "Poltava", it seems, apart from its proper worth, has what is needed for success: a respectable title, diverting contents, a new and popular subject.[5] I confess that I do not know what our public wants. Vyžigins, it seems![6] Do you know that 2,000 copies of that rubbish have been distributed? Either the public is growing stupid or it will decidedly *come to*, and say, with just indignation, who do they take me for? I have a request to make of you. If you have a few more spare copies of your portrait, give me one. D. Davydov[7] wheedled the one that you gave me earlier out of me, wanting to copy it, but instead kept the original and said simply: I shan't return it. You can justly say: they are tearing me apart.[8] Farewell, dear prince, I hope everyone is well in your house and that you are now calmer in your heart. Please convey my sincere respects to the princess.

E. Baratynskij

---

[1] Taken from *Starina i novizna* (1902), bk. 5, 45-46, checked against the original, preserved in *CGALI*. Dated on the basis of Puškin's leaving Moscow for Tiflis in early May 1829.

[2] A poem by Vjazemskij, published in the almanac *Podsnežnik* (April 4), 1829. The present was a separate reprint of the piece, which Vjazemskij had written in 1825. It is a lengthy poem of some three hundred lines. Puškin took a dozen lines from it as commentary to *Evgenij Onegin*, 7, 34. The station is not, of course, for railway passengers, but a stopping place, roadside inn or similar establishment on a stage route. The first locomotive did not leave Petersburg for Carskoe Selo until 1838.

[3] Puškin left in the first week of May, arriving in Tiflis, via Kaluga, Orel and the military road from Ekaterinoslav to Vladikavkaz, on May 27. He stayed there fifteen days. The C-in-C., Gen. I. F. Paskevič, gave him permission to ride to Erzerum with the Nižegorodskij Dragoons, in which his brother Lev was serving. On June 11, near the fortress of Gergeti, he met the coffin of Griboedov, who had been disfigured almost beyond recognition by a mob in Teheran. Three days later he attempted to take part in a skirmish with Turkish cavalry. He was back in Moscow by mid-September.

[4] *Poltava* was published in late March, 1829.

[5] "Popular" = 'to do with the people'.

[6] Bulgarin's *Ivan Vyžigin* (1829) was admittedly an uninspired historical novel; but its successors were worse.

[7] Denis Vasil'evič Davydov was a hero of the Napoleonic wars whose fame had been assured by his own pen, especially by his *Dnevnik partizanskix dejstvij 1812-ogo goda.* He was lionized in both capitals.

[8] See note 4 to letter 26.

29

To I. V. Kireevskij   (29 November, 1829; Moscow)[1]

My dearest friend,[2] give these verses to Maksimovič[3] and thank him on my behalf for his kind letter. I am not replying to him because I have no time, and am hurrying to send my quitrent to his almanac off to the post. In my last letter I unforgivably forgot to thank your mother for her intention to send me the Walter Scott novelty.[4] It seems that I already have it: it is *Charles le Téméraire*, is it not?[5] You will see from the enclosed verses that I have a new *poèma* on the loom, and an ultra-romantic one.[6] I am writing it headlong. Farewell, dear friend, I embrace you heartily and, of course, send my regards likewise to all your family,[7] which is very, very dear to me.

E. Baratynskij

[1] Taken from *Tatevskij sbornik S. A. Račinskogo* (St.P., 1899), 8. Ivan Vasil'evič Kireevskij (1806-1856) was a critic, journalist and Slavophile. In 1828, however, his Slavophilism was still in embryonic form. The relationship between him and Baratynskij is an interesting one. Idealism had some (limited) impact on the poet largely in the person of, and through the agency of, Kireevskij; see *Academy edition*, vol. 1, LXIX-LXXI; *1936 edition*, vol. 1, LXXXIII-XC. To his younger friend Baratynskij opened his mind and, sometimes, his heart, more fully than to any other man except Del'vig and, in later years, Putjata. Sheer weight of correspondence compensated for Kireevskij's absence, in 1830-1831, in Germany.

By 1824, Baratynskij's literary reputation was established; his fame was commonly connected, in the middle of that decade, with Puškin's. Kireevskij's literary début, on the other hand, was in 1828 ("Nečto o xaraktere poèzii Puškina", *Moskovskij vestnik*, 1828). In the first months of the relationship Baratynskij was already an established writer, he a novice. Yet there is no suggestion that Kireevskij found the friendship flattering. Other factors, moreover, may be recalled. In 1829, when the friendship developed, Baratynskij's popularity was declining among the general reading public, and even among Moscow and Petersburg *littérateurs*. Kireevskij, only six years his junior, still represented an alien (German-orientated) generation, and was the voice of that part of his generation who had studied Schelling to good effect. Baratynskij was conscious of the age-gap (see "Na posev lesa", 1840).

Kireevskij's interest in the older poet was aroused by the poem "Na smert' Gete"; but even in 1829 he liked Baratynskij for his own sake. From the first, Kireevskij offered advice, sympathy, encouragement and, above all, attention; Baratynskij's fame, still widespread in 1829, was in that year that of "a first-class elegiac" — exactly what it had been ten years earlier. Kireevskij could see the problem. The 'Schellingians' mounted their attacks; Kireevskij did not. On the contrary, he defended "Naložnica", which was almost universally attacked in other journals, in *Dennica* and *Evropeec*. Baratynskij, he declared, was a "European poet" in the same way that Puškin or de Vigny were. Baratynskij's 'Europeanism' was by no means as sound as Kireevskij cared to believe. Never did the poet express his opinion as to Russia's 'world-role', still less claim that Holy Rus' was to save and redeem world culture. Only occasional poems, "V dni bezgraničnyx uvlečenij" and "Na smert' Gete" chief among them, lent themselves to a Schellingian interpretation. Neither *schöne Seelen* nor the concept of perfect selfful-filment made a perceptible impression on Baratynskij. It was the notion of harmony that attracted him, briefly, to the German school — and already in 1826 (see letter 22) he could write ironically of "Moscow youth" which was enamoured of "the German aesthetic". Baratynskij's own life, in 1826, was dislocated; prospects of reconciliation and of harmony naturally appealed to him.

[2]   Lit. 'My soul '
[3]   Mixail Aleksandrovič Maksimovič (1804-1873), editor of *Dennica*.
[4]   "Your mother" had remarried; Elagina Avdot'ja Juškova (1789-1877) married first the critic's father, then Petrov.
[5]   Apparently an error. No work by Scott was published under this or a similar title.
[6]   "Cyganka", renamed after objections to the title "Naložnica", then renamed again — "Naložnica"".
[7]   Lit. '... to all your house'.

30

To P. A. Vjazemskij   (Late November, 1830; Moscow)[1]

I cannot argue with you, dear prince, no matter how much I might wish to. To stay in Ostaf'evo[2] is, for the time being, more sensible than to go to Moscow. My invitation was a little thoughtless, but was inspired by my strong desire to see you. Thank you for your friendly and flattering letter,

[1]   Taken from the original, preserved in the Baratynskij Archive, *CGALI*. Dated on the basis of the rising in Warsaw, which began on November 17, 1830.
[2]   The Vjazemskij estate outside Moscow, five miles from Podol'sk. Baratynskij refers to an outbreak of cholera, widespread in many provinces, including his native Tambov, throughout 1830 and 1831. Two months earlier, in mid-September, Puškin had been inconvenienced by the *cholera morbus* (as he thought it) (see A. S. Puškin, *Polnoe sobranie sočinenij*, 16 vols., vol. 14, Moscow, 1937-1949, 112-13). In fact the disease widespread throughout European Russia was not the comparatively mild *cholera morbus*, but the most virulent form of cholera, called Asiatic or Indian cholera. From the cities on the Volga the disease reached Moscow and, in early 1831, Petersburg. In Poland, the Grand-Duke Constantine and Dibič, C-in-C of the Russian forces suppressing the Polish uprising, both died of it. Both Vjazemskij and Baratynskij were lucky; seven thousand people died of it in Petersburg alone. For an excellent account of the outbreak, see C. M. Birrell, *The Life of the Rev. Richard Knill, of St. Petersburgh...* (London, 1860, 3rd ed.; reprinted by Oriental Research Partners, Cambridge, 1970).

but, believe me, you touched me more by your concern for me than by your favourable review of my new piece,[3] although I value your approval highly. I have already sent your stroll in the steppe[4] to Del'vig and, bearing in mind his celebrated lethargy, think that your poem will arrive in time. It is full of colour and feeling. Such poetry purifies the air better than chlorine. You cleaned my soul with it, and I am most grateful to you for sending it to *Northern Flowers* through me. I do not know what to reply to your proposal of publishing the Russian classics, or ancients. I have written little in prose, and no matter how many times I have taken it up, have always been unsuccessful.[5] My patience dries up on the second page. In all conscience I cannot answer for myself. I will settle down to work, and test my strength. Allow me to undertake Lomonosov. Not having a highly ingenious turn of mind, I think I shall succeed better with a serious article than with a playful one. As far as Tred'jakovskij is concerned, I wish to deprive neither myself nor the public of what you will say of him. Reading your letter, I seem to see with what a smile you wrote his name. How much news there is in Moscow! There is one piece of news of the greatest importance. Warsaw has risen and the Grand Duke[6] has been forced to leave it. But that is not all. With his small army, he has fallen into a trap. The Wista,[7] which is behind him, does not permit him to retire into Lithuania. Add to that the fact that Lithuania is also unreliable. The Lithuanian corps is formed entirely of Poles.[8] At most, a half will stay on the Russian side. The moment of decisive struggle has come, the outcome of which will have incalculable consequences. We need the greatest swiftness and energy now. After this news, all other news is secondary. You will hear, however (perhaps you already know it), that *The Literary Gazette* has been closed[9] because of a quatrain by Casimir de la Vigne,[10] probably on Bulgarin's instigation. Farewell, dear prince. What a pity it is that we are not living close to one another, but there is nothing to be done. My wife thanks the princess and you for remembering her, and is honoured.

Yours truly, E. Baratynskij

[3] "Naložnica". Which review Baratynskij has in mind is not clear. Extracts of the work were published in *Dennica* for 1830. Vjazemskij must have based his remarks on a few strophes only. However, Puškin seems to have known the whole *poèma* by January of the following year (see letter to Pletnev of January 7, 1831; *A. S. Puškin, 1962*, vol. 10, 11). Vjazemskij may therefore have seen a manuscript before committing himself to an opinion. In any event, his early view did not influence that of the majority; the *poèma* was attacked in *Teleskop* (1831, Pt. 1, no. 2, and Pt. 3, no. 10), in *Moskovskij telegraf* (1831, no. 6), in *Damskij žurnal* (1831, May, Pt. 34, 111), in *Girljanda* (1831, no. 13, 320-325), etc.

[4] "Progulka v stepi" was published in *Literaturnaja gazeta*, 1831, no. 3.

[5] A modesty justified, unfortunately, by the juvenile pieces "O zabluždenijax i istine" and "Istorija koketstva", as by the attempt at a tale *a l'Odoevskij* — "Persten'", published in Kireevskij's *Evropeec*, 1832, Pt. 1, no. 2, 165-187.

[6] Konstantin Pavlovič (1779-1831), Viceroy of Poland.

[7] The Wisła flows through Warsaw. Baratynskij reflected the general view of the Russian liberal gentry. Writing to Vjazemskij on June 1, 1831, Puškin described the recent events in Poland and the battle of Ostroleka in these terms: "Skrzynecki was in that battle. Our officers saw how he galloped up on his white horse, ... they saw how, wounded in the shoulder, he dropped his broadsword and tumbled off his horse... Then he began singing 'Poland Has Not Yet Perished', and his suite began to chime in... All this is fine in a poetic sense. But all the same they must be throttled, and our slowness is tormenting. For us the Polish rebellion is a family affair, an ancient, hereditary dissension; we cannot judge it by the reactions of Europeans..."

[8] An extraordinary exaggeration.

[9] The ban came into effect on November 15, 1830. It struggled on, under the editorship of O. M. Somov, into 1831, then died.

[10] The story is an unpleasant one. Del'vig, as editor of *Literaturnaja gazeta*, had attacked the official nationalism (*oficial'naja narodnost'*) propagated by certain rival periodicals. Using as a pretext the fact that Del'vig had published a piece by the French poet Casimir Delavigne honouring the memory of victims of the July Revolution, Beckendorff called him to his office and threatened him, Puškin and Vjazemskij with Siberian exile, were the "direction" of the journal not immediately changed. Shaken, Del'vig relinquished the editorship to Orest Somov; within three weeks he was dead.

31

To N. V. Putjata   (June?, 1831; Kazan')[1]

I am late in replying to your letter, dear Putjata, but you will forgive me when you learn that I have only recently received it and that it was sent on to me from Moscow to Kazan', where I am now living with all my family. Thank you for delivering "The Concubine" to the addresses[2] and for your comments. I will not deny that there are certain careless lines in "The Concubine", even bad lines, but believe me, in general the author of "Eda" made great progress in his latest work. I am not speaking of the difficulties overcome, of the genre of *poèma* itself, full of movement, like a novel in prose; compare the dramatic part with the descriptive: you will see that the conversations in "The Concubine" are less constrained, more natural, the descriptions simpler and more precise. There are, as a matter of fact, far more *bad* passages in "Eda" than in "The Concubine". One may criticize the verse, the expression in the latter; but in "Eda" there are whole tirades, for example, the whole conversation between the

[1] Taken from *Russkij arxiv*, 1867, bk. 2, 280-281. Dated on the basis of Baratynskij's having left Kazan' for Kajmary, with his family, early in July 1831.

[2] The addresses are unknown.

Hussar and Eda in the first canto. Usually my most recent work seems to me worse than earlier ones, but on re-reading "The Concubine" I am always struck by the lightness and aptness of its style compared with that of my earlier *poèmy*. If a certain carelessness is discernible in "The Concubine", it is made up for by the fact that my labour[3] is quite unnoticable; and that was necessary in a *poèma* full of embarrassing details, with which one had to deal completely successfully[4] or the thing was better not attempted. I have been rambling, dear friend. Forgive my arguing with you. You know that I willingly agree with critics when I find them just; but I do not agree with your view. I would have liked to say something amusing to you, but I live in complete seclusion and can share nothing with you but my thoughts. I see from the papers that cholera is not dying down where you are;[5] but I know by experience that one can probably escape it by eating moderately and making efforts not to catch cold. I trust that you will not be its victim, and that God may allow us to embrace once again. Farewell. My address: to me by name, in Kazan'.

E. Baratynskij

[3] I.e., the labour that went into it. The quality of genius is not strained.
[4] Lit. 'out of which it was necessary to come a total victor...'
[5] See note 2 to letter 30; excited by rumour and counter-rumour of coming emancipation and decimated by the cholera and grain shortage, serfs rioted in several provinces in the summer and autumn of 1830. In Tambov, troops refused to fire into the crowd; see *Tatevskij arxiv*, 25.

32

To P. A. Pletnev   (June, 1831; Kajmary)[1]

When I received your letter, dear Pletnev,[2] I was packing for a long journey, so did not reply then. I am writing to you now not from Moscow

[1] Taken from *Russkaja starina*, 1904, June, 518-519, where it is taken from the book *Pomošč' golodajuščim* (Moscow, 1892), 259-260; there is a copy in the Saltykov-Ščedrin Public Library, Leningrad, where this version was checked.
[2] Petr Aleksandrovič Pletnev (1792-1865) was the son of a deacon. He studied mathematics and physics in Petersburg before changing courses, and taught in various ladies' institutes and private schools. By chance, he was noticed by a member of the Empress's inner court circle, and appointed tutor in literature to the Imperial children. In 1832, he was appointed Professor of Russian Literature at St. Petersburg University, and eight years later became its *rektor*. He was amiable, helpful to all, an aesthete, and Baratynskij's friend for twenty-five years. After the poet's death, his widow and children had good reason to thank Pletnev for his unfailing kindness and sure advice;

but from a village 20 versts from Kazan'. I am further from you in distance, but no further in heart. Your letter disturbed me.[3] It breathes disillusion and despondency. It is with sharp pangs of conscience that I think that I myself have helped somewhat to reduce you to this low state of spirits. Content in my heart with a warm and friendly recollection of you, I did not trouble to assure you of it and, so it seemed, forgot about an old friend. It is terrible to me to think that you, remembering me, said to yourself: that is how insensitive and ungrateful people are! Yet I was guilty only of laziness, putting off until the morrow what should be done today. The loss of Del'vig[4] is irreplacable. If we meet at some time, if we sit down together at your table one Saturday, God! how alone we shall still be. Dear friend, Del'vig's death has shown us what the irrevocable past is really like, which we would guess at with sad inspiration – what a deserted world is, which we spoke about not knowing the full meaning of our phrases. I have not yet set to work on the life of Del'vig.[5] His death is too fresh in my memory. Not only grief but also thoughts are necessary; and I am still unable to bring them into order. Let us speak of you. Is it possible that you have left literature entirely? I know that poetry is not contained in the dead letter, that one may be silent and be a poet; but I am sorry that you have abandoned art, which consoles us for life's sadnesses better than any philosophy. To express a feeling is to resolve it, to control it. That is why the gloomiest of poets are able to preserve their spirits. Take up the pen again, my dear Pletnev; do not betray your vocation. We will complete our life's labour with fortitude. Talent is an obligation. One must use it notwithstanding any obstacles, and of those the greatest is laziness. Farewell, my dear friend. I have become a preacher. Attend to my admonitions, and I will attend to yours. Thank you for your praises of "The Concubine".[6] They consoled me for the hostility of other critics.[7] I embrace you with all my heart. Write to me when you find time. My regards to Puškin. My address – the same, in Kazan'.

E. Baratynskij

---

see my article, "P. A. Pletnyov and N. L. Baratynskaya: Unpublished Correspondence", *Scando-Slavica*, XV (1969), 35-45. Pletnev, as a friend of Baratynskij, reviewed his work favourably, but justly; see "Pis'mo k Grafine S.I.S. o russkix poètax", *Severnye cvety* (1825), 3-80, and "O stixotvorenijax Baratynskogo", *ibid.* (1828), 301-11. Pletnev was liked and trusted by Puškin, who used him, and occasionally abused him, as a reliable literary executor.

[3] The letter has not survived.

[4] Del'vig died on January 14, 1831. By a wonderful coincidence, Del'vig died on the anniversary of the death of the fictional Lenskij; and the wake commemorating Del'vig's death (which produced a fit of grief in Baratynskij; see *A. S. Puškin, 1962,*

vol. 10, 14) was held by Baratynskij, Puškin, Vjazemskij and Jazykov, in a Moscow restaurant, on January 27, 1831 — six years to the day before Puškin's duel with d'Anthès.

⁵ As early as January 31, 1831, Puškin could tell Pletnev of Baratynskij's intention to write Del'vig's biography; see *A. S. Puškin, 1962*, vol. 10, 16. If, as is most probable, Baratynskij started work on the life, the completed fragments have not survived; see also letter 41.

⁶ Perhaps in *Severnye cvety* for 1831, perhaps in a lost letter.

⁷ Hostile articles appeared in 1831 by Senserskij, Ju. R-n, Polevoj, Nadeždin, P. I. Šalikov and D. V. L'vov, *inter alia* in *Girljanda, Syn otečestva i severnyj arxiv, Moskovskij telegraf, Teleskop, Damskij žurnal* and *Listok* (Pt. 1, no. 13, 320-325; Pt. 142, no. 1, 53-63; vol. 38, no. 5, 235-243; Pt. 3, no. 10, 228-39; May, Pt. 34, 111 and no. 39, 2-3).

33

To I. V. Kireevskij   (June, 1831; Kajmary)¹

How are you, my dear Kireevskij, and what are you doing? Is your novel progressing?² By the way – about the novel: I have thought a lot about it recently, and this is what I think. All earlier novelists are unsatisfactory for our time because they all adhered to one system or another. Some are spiritualists, others – materialists. Some depict only the physical realities of human nature, others see only its spirituality. It is necessary to combine the two forms in one – to write an eclectic novel, in which man would be depicted in the one form and the other. Although everything is said, it is said separately. Drawing the realities together, we see them in a new form, a new light. There you have my reflections in short and in freemasons' language. I am doing nothing for the present. For the time being, trees and foliage divert me as much in the countryside as people in the city. I ride every day, in a word I lead a life with which only Ramix³ could be satisfied. Farewell, my dear friend, I embrace you; embrace Jazykov for me. Do not forget about the almanac.

Your E. Baratynskij

I read the highly flattering and highly generalized analysis of "The Concubine" in *The Literary Gazette*.⁴ That was a friend's review.⁵ What do the enemies say? If you have something, be kind and send it. I intend to reply to the critics. My wife sends you her regards.

¹ Taken from *Tatevskij sbornik S. A. Račinskogo* (St.P., 1899), 10-11.

² *Dve žizni*, never completed.

³ A mutual acquaintance, a servant?

⁴ Baratynskij politely refers to Kireevskij's habit of avoiding explicit examples, quotations, facts — a trait common to most Russian 'Schellingians'.

⁵ Baratynskij is aware of the reality of the situation; see introductory notes to letter 29.

34

To I. V. Kireevskij   (July, 1831; Kajmary)[1]

I am answering you extremely promptly, and therefore ask you to take this
scrap as a note and not as a letter. Thank you for sending the good news
of your mother's health. I hope that soon it will be quite sound. Concerning my business affairs,[2] I could give you a very brief reply: I could
say, do what you wish, and I would be calm; but I know that you are an
extremely conscientious fellow and that, should something go wrong, you
would be more vexed than I. For this reason I will say that, as regards
Širjaev,[3] I agree with you. Concerning Kol'čugin,[4] I am thinking of
letting him have the copies at less than R. 8, at 7.50 or even 7 if he will
take 100 at once.

   It seems to me that we are both right about the novel: any approach is
good, provided only that it is clear and forceful. I wrote to you more
about the novel in general than about your novel; I think, however, that
my thoughts will suggest something to you, perhaps the details of a
certain scene. I know very well that one must not re-create what has once
been created. Write to tell me how you find Gnedič[5]. I confess that I am
sorry I shall not see him. I loved him, and that feeling has not yet cooled.
Perhaps I should now find something comic in him: what a thing! It is
pleasant to see the bell-tower of the village in which one was born,
though it no longer seems as high as in one's childhood. I am doing nothing
for the present: I ride out and, like you, read Rousseau. I will write to you
about him in a day or two: he has aroused many thoughts and feelings
in me. Certainly a remarkable man and more sincere than I thought at
first. Everything that he says about himself no doubt *was*, perhaps not
in the order in which he tells it. His *Confessions* are a tremendous gift to
mankind. I embrace you.

                                                        E. Baratynskij

PS. I have received the money.

[1] Taken from that source also, 11-12.
[2] Affairs connected with the sale of the edition of "Naložnica" published in the
the spring of 1831. Like the collection of 1827 and *Sumerki*, the collection of 1842,
Naložnica: sočinenie E. Baratynskogo, was published (separately) in the printing shop
of Avgust Semen. It was of 90 pages in 12°, and sold for ten roubles. Censor's permission was granted as of March 20.
   A great deal is known of the prices of books and journals in Russia in the period
1810-1850; such book-sellers and publishers as Smirdin and Plavil'ščikov produced
regular catalogues and lists of works available (*Rospis' rossijskim knigam dlja čtenija iz
biblioteki A. Smirdina, Rospis' knigam za 1822g, 1823g*, etc.). A selection of data from

these sources may be seen in André Meynieux's *Pouchkine, Homme de Lettres* (Paris, 1966), 471-481.

Ten roubles for the 1827 verse collection and for *Naložnica* (1831) was an average price. According to the Smirdin list for 1829, collections of verse by Del'vig and Kozlov were also 10 R., while vol. 1 of Venevitinov's verse (1829) sold for a more modest 6 R. *Boris Godunov* also cost 10 R. in 1831 (*op. cit.*, 485). By 1831, however, the effect of a huge increase in the Russian reading public (between 1824 and 1834, the numbers quadrupled) was being reflected in a steady drop in prices. In 1832, chapters 7 and 8 of *Evgenij Onegin* sold for 10 R. in Ol'xin's shop (catalogue 5364), but five years later changed hands for only two. *Baxčiserajskij fontan*, in its fifth edition by 1831, sold for 5 R., and *Dušenka*, in its tenth edition in 1832, for 4 R.

³ A Muscovite bookseller.

⁴ Ditto; booksellers and publishers tended, in the first half of the nineteenth century, to be one and the same people. Few were more successful, in Russia, than were Avgust Semen and Aleksandr Smirdin. It is interesting that Baratynskij should think a hundred copies of his "Naložnica" a considerable number — more, perhaps, than Kol'čugin would have taken as a normal first consignment. True, Kol'čugin specialized in other fields than poetry, and may have had his own reasons for thinking that the *poèma* would not prove popular with his clientèle. In all events, the numbers involved were low, and the prices high.

⁵ Nikolaj Ivanovič Gnedič (1784-1833), celebrated as the translator of *The Iliad* (1829), classicist, scholar and poet, was a sick man in the summer of 1831; he did not recover. Baratynskij deeply admired him; see "N. I. Gnediču" (1823), especially the final quatrain.

35

To I. V. Kireevskij   (6 August, 1831; Kajmary)¹

Why are you silent, dear Kireevskij? Your silence disturbs me. I know you too well to ascribe it to coolness; I have not the right to attribute it to laziness. Are you well, and all your family? I simply do not know what to think. I am in the most hypochondriac of moods, and one question revolves obstinately in my mind: why do you not write? I need a letter from you.² I do not know what to write to you about. I have already been in my Kazan' village one month. At first I busied myself with the estate, talked to bailiffs and elders. I have a lawsuit on, and discussed it with judges and secretaries. You can imagine how gay that was. Now I am resting, but I do not yet know how to use my leisure. One thought follows another and I cannot settle on any one. My imagination is strained,³ its creations are vivid but wilful, and my lazy mind cannot

¹ Taken from that same source, 15-17.

² A literal truth. Baratynskij became almost physically, certainly emotionally, dependent on Kireevskij. 1831 was a year of intense correspondence between the two.

³ It is not clear whether or not Baratynskij regrets this; perhaps for "strained" one might read 'taut'.

bring them into order. There you have my psychological confession. On the road and, in part, at home, I reread Rousseau's *Heloïse*.[4] How was it that that novel seemed impassioned? It is amazingly cold. With difficulty I found two truly moving passages and two or three expressions straight from the heart. Saint-Preux's letters[5] are better than Julie's, there is more naturalness in them; but in the main they are a moral treatise, not the letters of two lovers. There is no dramatic truth whatever in Rousseau's novel,[6] nor the least dramatic talent. You will say that it is not necessary in a novel that has no pretensions to drama – a purely analytic novel; but this is a novel in letters, and in a letter's style the author's voice should be discernible: in its way it is the same as a conversation, and see how superior the author of *Clarissa*[7] is to Rousseau. It is plain that Rousseau had neither the depiction of characters nor even the expression of passion in mind, but chose the novel form in order to express his own views on religion and to investigate a few subtle questions of morality. It is clear that he wrote *Heloïse* in old age: he knows the emotions, determines them accurately, but in his heroes that very self-knowledge is cold, for it is not in keeping with their years. The novel is bad; Rousseau is good as a moralist, a dialectician, a metaphysician, but ... certainly not as a creator. His characters are faceless, and although he says in his *Confessions* that they presented themselves clearly to his mind's eye I do not believe it. Rousseau knew and understood only himself, observed only himself, and all his characters are Jean-Jacques, some in trousers, some in skirts. Farewell, my dear friend. I share what I can with you – my thoughts. Write, for God's sake. Give my regards to all your family and to Jazykov. I hope that I shall soon stop worrying about you and only be a little angry.

---

[4] *La Nouvelle Heloïse* produced an enormous impact in Russia; see V. I. Kulešov, *Literaturnye svjazi Rossii i zapadnoj Evropy v XIX veke* (Moscow, 1965), 176-196. From this and the succeeding letters, it is clear that Baratynskij censures Rousseau for failing in that some aesthetic undertaking that forms the basis of his own work — the expression of his own views on questions touching all men of all times and races. Baratynskij chooses to judge Rousseau only as a novelist, — not as a "metaphysician" (as which, he concedes, Rousseau excels), nor as an influential thinker.

Like Rousseau, Baratynskij was preoccupied with the quest for happiness, and sought it — briefly — through the free play of the emotions. His youthful imagination was brilliant (see letters 5 and 6); something of Rousseau's emotional satiety re-echoes in "Dve doli" (1823). The treatment of the theme of inevitable unhappiness, however, is very different. Emotional exhaustion does not imply mental immaturity. Seldom in Baratynskij's verse are there traces of Rousseauesque pride in suffering. Not unlike Constant's Adolphe, Baratynskij "*arrive en même temps au dernier dégré de la langeur vitale et de la lucidité intellectuelle*" (G. Rudler, *La Jeunesse de Benjamin Constant, 1764-1794*, Paris, 1909, 384). (Baratynskij, however, does not become aware of the folly of emotion as an afterthought.)

Rousseau is censured for being one-sided. When Rousseau's work appeals to Baratynskij, it is in those places where his "dreams are vivid". Presumably, therefore, the bulk of Rousseau's writing, which is nothing if not imaginative, seems to Baratynskij based on dreams that are *not* vivid, in other words, which are not sympathetic to him. Not only Rousseau's "dreams", however, but also their presentation is alien to Baratynskij. This is to be felt in the present letter. An ability to "parade the wounded heart in a sling" (with which an Irish girl is said to have charged Chateaubriand) stems from Rousseau, not from his books. Far from making a pageant of his wounded sensibilities, Baratynskij strove to imitate the actions of an Arnold; ("Among us one / Who most has suffered, takes dejectedly / His seat upon the intellectual throne...", "The Scholar Gipsy", 11.182-184). Scornful of those who, as Goethe had it, "write as though they were ill, and the world a hospital" (letter to Eckermann of September 24, 1827), Baratynskij seems to have believed that "it is fitting to show openly to all folk the fair and sweet things allotted us; but (that) if any dire misfortune sent of heaven befalleth man, it is fitting to shroud it in darkness" (Pindar; my translation of a fragment given in Stobaeus, *Florian*, CIX, 1). It was because Rousseau had no compunction in sharing his grief and disillusionment with the first-comer — or first-reader — that Baratynskij had little patience with him.

⁵   Saint-Preux, main character of *La Nouvelle Héloïse* (1763).

⁶   The novel was not, one may say, a drama. The charge stands, however.

⁷   Charles Richardson (1689-1761), author of *Pamela, Clarissa Harlowe*, was chiefly known to Baratynskij's generation through French translations (as were Fielding's *Amelia* and all the works of Defoe); see M. P. Alekseev, "Fielding in the Russian Language", cited in *Meždunarodnye svjazi russkoj literatury* (Moscow, 1963), 69. Baratynskij was certainly acquainted with Richardson through French translations; in a letter to his mother he writes that he has purchased, for the sum of 25 roubles, the last copy of *Clarissa Harlowe* in the shop, probably the Letourneur version of 1785-1786; see *Tatevskij arxiv*, 32.

36

To I. V. Kireevskij   (August, 1831; Kajmary)[1]

Your friendship, dear Kireevskij, is part of my domestic happiness; the picture of that happiness would be far from complete, were I to forego our conversations about you, the pleasure with which we read your letters, the sincerity with which we love you and with which, to our delight, you repay us. We both see a dear brother in you, and draw you into our family life in our thoughts. You will not leave it, and are always in our company, always under our roof in our dreams of the future, when we arrange them to our fancy. You are the first person of all I have known to whom I can open my heart without constraint: which means that no one ever inspired me with such trust in their heart and character. I would have described our country life for you, but am not in the mood. I will tell you briefly that we drink tea, take lunch and supper an hour earlier

[1]   Taken from that same source, 12-14.

than in Moscow. There you have the frame of our existence. Place in it walks, rides, conversations; place in it what there is no name for: that shared feeling, that sum of impressions in us, that forces us to wake up cheerful, to walk about cheerfully – the paradise of family happiness – and you will have a fairly accurate idea of my way of life. "The Concubine" I leave completely in your charge. I await your review with impatience.[2] Send it when you have finished it. You can briefly hint at the shortcomings of "Boris"[3] and enlarge on its virtues. In that way you will be justified in your own eyes and in those of others. I do not entirely agree with you that the style of *Ioanna*[4] served as a model for that of "Boris". Žukovskij could teach Puškin only the use of unrhymed verse, and not even that, for Puškin did not follow Žukovskij's methods, his constant observance of the caesura. The style of *Ioanna* is good in itself; so, too, is that of "Boris". In the style of "Boris" one sees a true feeling for antiquity, the feeling that creates the poetry of Puškin's tragedy, while in *Ioanna* the style is good in a general way. Farewell, my dear friend, I embrace you tightly. Write to us. My wife is most grateful to you for your friendly greetings. I always write to you for both of us, however. Embrace Jazykov for me, I am very glad that he is recovering. I want to see you both very much and will perhaps bring myself to Moscow for a day or two if my health allows. Do not forget to give my regards to Gnedič.

E. Baratynskij

[2] "Obozrenie russkoj slovesnosti za 1831 God", comprising a study of *Boris Godunov*, a review of "Naložnica" and comments on several other works, was published in *Evropeec*, 1832, no. 2. In it "Naložnica" was praised.

[3] *Boris Godunov* was not a *nouveau arrivé* — the piece had been begun in December 1824 and was completed on November 7 of the following year.

[4] Baratynskij refers to Žukovskij's translation of Schiller's *Die Jungfrau von Orleans* by its heroine. Žukovskij did *not* give a literal rendering.

37

To I. V. Kireevskij   (21 September, 1831; Kajmary)[1]

I am replying this once to your two letters, dear Kireevskij, they came together. Do not be surprised at that: the Moscow post arrives in Kazan' twice a week, and we send into town from our village only once a week. Thank you for the troubles that you took over "The Concubine". Perhaps

[1] Taken from that same source, 19-21.

it will sell out in the winter. However, its success or failure is all one to me now. I have somehow grown cool towards its fortunes. Your intention to publish a journal has made me truly happy. I am only afraid that it will remain one of our thousand plans that stayed – plans. If the thing is realised, then I am your reliable[2] and diligent helper, the more so because everything inclines me towards prose. I hope in a year to give you two or three tales and to help you to conduct a lively polemic. I have not read the criticisms of "The Concubine": I do not receive any periodicals. If you could send me the issue of *The Telegraph* in which the objection to my foreword is printed, I would certainly reply, and reply efficiently and at length. I have thought over my subject even more since "The Concubine" appeared in print, have considered it and all questions touching it, and hope to resolve those questions while at no point contradicting my original propositions. My article would be suitable for your periodical. I will keep your issue of *The Telegraph* and send it back as soon as the article is ready. You are mistaken in thinking me an implacable critic of Rousseau; on the contrary, he has completely captivated me. I criticize only the *novel* in *Heloïse*, in the same way that one may criticize the form of Byron's *poèmy*. Byron and Rousseau used once to be compared, and I find the comparison most just. In the works of the one and of the other, no independence of imagination is to be found, only expression of their individuality. Both are poets of self; but Byron gives himself up utterly to contemplation of himself; Rousseau, born with more discriminating taste,[3] needs to deceive himself; he moralizes, and in moralizing expresses the needs of his own nervous, delicate heart. In *Heloïse* the wish to demonstrate his lofty understanding of man's moral perfection, and brilliantly to resolve a few difficult problems concerning the conscience, oblige him to forget dramatic probability. By its nature, love is an exclusive emotion and tolerates no sharing, and for that reason *Heloïse*, in which Rousseau gives himself over more often to moralizing than to description of the passions, produces such a strange, unsatisfactory impression. We see in the *Confessions* that his love for Mme Houdetot inspired him to write *Heloïse*; but from the disproportionate part that morality and philosophy (Rousseau's most personal possessions) play in it, we feel that the ideal of Saint-Lambert's mistress always yielded, in his imagination, to that of Jean-Jacques. It is in the make-up of Rousseau's heart,

---

[2]   Or 'faithful'.

[3]   The charge is a subtle one. Baratynskij impresses on Kireevskij that it is of *La Nouvelle Héloïse* that he speaks, not of its author; the distinction is a tenuous one in the present context, however.

rather than in the make-up of his novel, that one finds the latter's shortcomings. I like *Heloïse* less than his other works. The novel, I insist, is a
form completely alien to his genius. Whereas in *Heloïse* every page
annoys me, and even its beauties vex me, all his other works invincibly
captivate me. The warmth of his speech pierces my heart, his sincere love
of good touches me, his irritable sensitivity communicates itself to me.
You see how I have rambled with you. My wife, who is very fond of you,
sends you her regards. I embrace you.

E. Baratynskij

38

To N. M. Jazykov   (Late September, 1831; Kajmary)[1]

Thank you for your postscript to me, dear Jazykov. It was a great
triumph (alas) of your indolence, and a real proof of friendship. Having
taken my place under Germes,[2] you must replace me fully. I served two
years with outstanding zeal, for which I earned even promotion in rank.
Question Kireevskij about my feats in the service: I am sure that it will
enflame you to gratifying emulation.[3] It seems that the god of poets is now
not Apollo, but Hermes: besides you and me, Vjazemskij once served
under him. How can we write him some verses, praising him well because
even the Chancery of Furs turned into a Helicon under his direction? By
the way – about verses: Somehow I have abandoned them, and have only
prosaic plans in my head. This is very sad.

> Once, as a boy, I would awaken in the forest
> An echo with my ringing cry,
> And the true response in the wild forest

---

[1] Taken from *Istoriko-literaturnyj sbornik, posvjaščennyj V. I. Sreznevskomu* (Leningrad, 1924), 12-13. Baratynskij learned of Kireevskij's intention to publish a journal
on or about September 21 (see letter 37). This letter may thus be dated late September,
possibly early October, 1831.
   Nikolaj Mixajlovič Jazykov (1803-1846), greatly overestimated by Puškin, was more
justly rated by Baratynskij a fine but not first-class poet. The respect that each felt for
the other, however, was real. To Baratynskij, as to Puškin, Del'vig, Belinskij, Jazykov's
was essentially an energetic muse, and Jazykov the poet of youthful passions. Although
uneven, his verse is, indeed, warm-blooded, and bespeaks its author's temperamental
fuòco. Jazykov was also subject to periods of black depression — a thing that Baratynskij could understand.
[2] The head of the Chancery of Furs and messenger of the gods; a pun.
[3] The irony is conscious.

Perturbed me and made me merry.
There came another time,
And rhyme captured the youth,
Replacing the forest's echo
Game of verses, golden game!
How once sounds, answering sounds,
Indulged me!
But all things pass: I grow cold
Even to verses' harmony
And as I do not hail the forest groves,
So I seek not consonant words.[4]

This is the only piece that I have written since I parted from you, and in it I tried to express my sadness. What are you doing and will you soon be writing verse? Send what you write. It will inspire me to write.

Kireevskij is undertaking a periodical. The news of this has cheered me greatly. We are going to help him with all our strength: things will certainly take a turn for the better. Farewell, I embrace you as a friend.

E. Baratynskij

[4] First published in the verse collection of 1835, *Stixotvorenija Evgenija Baratynskogo: dve časti* (censor's permission as of March 7, 1833; printed in the shop of the Censorship Committee), 240.
The original may be consulted in Puškinskij Dom, 26322/CLXXXIX b. 11, 1.102.

39

To I. V. Kireevskij   (8 October, 1831; Kajmary)[1]

Thank you for the verses by Puškin and Žukovskij.[2] I would have liked to write them out, but you anticipated me. I had read the verses by Žukovskij in *Northern Flowers*, and could not guess the author. The unusual rhythms and conspicuous firmness of the style struck me, but the familiar tone put

[1] Taken from *Tatevskij sbornik S. A. Račinskogo*, 21-22.
[2] Baratynskij speaks of the brochure, or pamphlet, entitled *Na vzjatie Varšavy. Tri stixotvorenija V. Žukovskogo i A. Puškina* (St.P., 1831). The poems were Žukovskij's "Staraja pesnja na novyj lad" and Puškin's "Klevetnikam Rossii" and "Borodinskaja godovščina". It is an early example of Puškin's verse being adapted and adopted for purposes of propaganda. Its value in that respect has not diminished even in the present day; *Poltava* was published twice between 1937 and 1939, in which years also appeared A. K. Tolstoj's historical trilogy (published separately for the first time under the Bolsheviks), and Radiščev's heroic verse. All these works deal with victories over foreigners.

all thoughts of Žukovskij out of mind. I care for the first poem by
Puškin more than the second. The issue is stated in it and the proper
viewpoint given from which our war with Poland should be seen. You
underline the line: Gleaming like a steel bristle.[3] Probably you find it too
recherché. Perhaps you are right, but it is strong and picturesque. I have
already answered you regarding the periodical. Set to work and God be
with you. As far as the title is concerned, it seems to me that it would be
best of all to choose one that meant precisely nothing and so would have
no pretensions. *The European*, incomprehensible to the public, will be
taken in a pejorative sense by the journalists; and why arm them prematurely? Is it not possible to call the journal *The Northern Messenger*, *Orion*,
or something capricious but insignificant too, like *Yellow Dwarf*, which
the Bonapartists published under Louis XVIII?[4] You expect too much of
me, and I wonder if I shall fulfil your hopes. Of one thing I can assure
you: assiduousness. Your periodical greatly moves me to action. I have
written a few more small pieces in verse, besides those which I sent to you.
Now I am writing a short drama, my first attempt in that genre,[5] which,
no matter how bad, will serve for a periodical. I shall probably finish
it this week and will send it to you. Do not speak of it to anyone, but
read it and tell me your opinion. I will place it in a periodical without my
name. I am not telling you my most recent plans out of superstition.
What you have boasted of already you never write. I am very curious to
know what you will say of Zagoskin's novels.[6] All his works show talent
and stupidity at the same time. Zagoskin is an extremely curious psychological phenomenon. Send me your article as soon as you have written it.
I will help you in a concrete manner when I move to Moscow. I must
write in a hurry in order to write a great deal. I need to give myself up to
journalism as to a conversation, with all the liveliness of question and
answer, otherwise I am too demanding of myself, and this exactingness
often makes me cool towards my own good thoughts. In all events, all
that I manage to write in my seclusion will belong to your periodical.
Farewell, my regards to your people.

E. Baratynskij

Tell Jazykov that Rozen[7] is angry with him for not only not sending him
his last year's verses but not even replying to his letter. He complains
about this often and even movingly.

---

[3] Or 'Pike'; line 41 of "Klevetnikam Rossii" (1831).
[4] Louis XVIII had died in 1824.
[5] The piece has not survived, unless it is a mention of "Otryvok", published in

Severnye cvety for 1832, 70, as "Ceny iz poèmy 'Vera i neverie'". The time of writing is correct — late 1831; but the piece was, or was to have been, a *poèma*, not a drama — although the lay-out of the existing fragment is dramatic. It is mainly on the fragment that E. A. Bobrov rests assertions, in a curious article entitled "Iz poèzii E. A. Baratyn-skogo" (*Varšavskij dnevnik*, May 1914, no. 143, 2-3), that (a) Baratynskij was irreligious, or had atheistic leanings, and that (b) his wife, who is the 'ona' of "Otryvok", strove to lead him "onto the true and narrow path of Christian virtue". Part of the final strophe, spoken by 'ona', is engraved on the poet's tombstone in the Aleksandr-Nevskij Monastery's '19th-century', i.e. Tixvinskij, Cemetery. It is hopelessly out of context and inappropriate.

⁶ An article to be published in *Evropeec*; Mixail Nikolaevič Zagoskin (1789-1852) was the author of a number of historical or 'period' novels, including *Jurij Miloslavskij* (1829) and *Roslavlev* (1831).

⁷ Baron Egor Fedorovič Rozen (1800-1860) was a talented journalist and the publisher of *Carskoe selo* (1830) and of *Al'ciona* (1831), two short-lived almanacs, to which Baratynskij contributed, and which collapsed for want of subscribers. Baratynskij's contribution to the former, in particular, was generous; he gave Rozen four poems — "Èpigramma" ("V vostoržennom nevežestve svoem..."), "Muza", "K. A. Sverbeevoj" and a further epigram ("Čto pol'zy vam ot šumnyx vašix prenij?"), which appeared on pp. 7, 94, 133 and 140.

40

To I. V. Kireevskij   (26 October, 1831; Kajmary)¹

In society I have often experienced that dullness of which you speak. I have been angry at myself, but admit that I had a good opinion of myself also: I have reproached myself with stupidity, especially when comparing myself with those distinguished in the skill I lacked. To console you still more in your grief (I say grief jokingly), I will tell you that never did mortal shine so in parlour games and especially in secretary² as Vasilij L'vovič Puškin and even his brother Sergej L'vovič.³ This latter, to the question: What difference is there between Mr Puškin and the sun? replied: both make one grimace.⁴ However, there is nothing to be said: although we peer in at society, we are not society people. Our mind has been differently formed, and society's ways are not ours. For us society conversation is a learned labour, a dramatic production, because we are alien to the real life, the real passions of society. I will note one more thing:

---

¹ Taken from that same source, 23-24.
² Drawing-room games.
³ A game of questions and answers, *secrétaire*, gave the poet's uncle, who was by natural inclination a *bon vivant* and after-dinner speaker, the chance to air his store of anecdotes and show his repartee. Sergej was Puškin's father (1770-1848).
⁴ See note 3 to letter 28.

that ease[5] that makes us skilful in society is a quality natural to those who are limited. It is given them by self-sufficiency, always inseparable from stupidity. People of another kind obtain it by experience. Having compared their strong points with those of others for a long time, they at last notice their own superiority and give themselves free rein, not so much from a feeling of their own merit as from a conviction of the worthlessness of the greater part of their fellows. I am not sending my attempt at drama yet because it needs to be re-written, and my copyist[6] is still in bed. Thank you for the money and for Villemain.[7] I felt easier when I caught sight of that dirty volume,[8] which has tormented me pretty well. I have already read two parts: there is much that is good and well expressed; but Villemain often gives out what was known to the Germans long ago, and which they discovered, as something new and his own observation. Much is written only for a success and for the applause of the factions. One more remark: the affectation of atticism is often noticeable with Villemain – the affectation of the very best tone. His modest reservations are monotonous, in the first place, and rather recherché, in the second. You feel that he is admiring his own social-aesthetic meekness.[9] This does not prevent his work from being most diverting. Regarding Guizot,[10] I will tell you that I have no money now. If you can lend me the necessary amount until January, take it; if not, tell Urbain[11] that I do not need Guizot, or ask him to wait for his money. Farewell; all my family send you their regards. I shall write to Jazykov by the next post. For the time being, I embrace you.

E. Baratynskij

[5]   The nearest approximation, perhaps, to the untranslatable French.
[6]   The poet's wife.
[7]   Abel-François Villemain (1790-1870), French critic and historian. It seems that Baratynskij is referring to a *Cours de la Littérature Française* (1828). Another possibility, however, is M. Villemain's *Discours et Mélanges Littéraires* (1823), from which the poet took the comparison between Rousseau and Byron (letter 37; p. 521 in the Ladvocat edition of Villemain, Paris, 1823). Here, however, there are no Schellingian traits whatever. There were many Villemains in Russian libraries of the period. Henri Villemain saw fit, in 1803, to produce four volumes of translation from Heinrich J. Lafontaine (1758-1831), notably from *Die Familie von Halden* (1789). He redeemed himself in 1816 with a passable translation of Jane Austen's *Mansfield Park* (*Le Parc de Mansfield, ou Les Trois Cousins*). (Actually, there are two sisters and a cousin.)
[8]   Physically.
[9]   *Sic.* Baratynskij does not express himself clearly here.
[10]   François Guizot (1787-1874), historian and statesman, author of *Histoire de la Civilization en Europe* (1828), *Histoire de la Civilization en France* (1829-1832).
[11]   A French bookseller in Moscow.

41

To I. V. Kireevskij   (November, 1831; Kajmary)[1]

Thank you for your friendly congratulations and amiable jokes. I shall take you at your word, however: *The European* must come out without fail in the year of my Mašen'ka's birth;[2] and if, when she is twelve, she is of a condition to understand your lectures, I ask you to concern yourself with her education.[3] It is not a bad thing that my poem was bought. I have sent Puškin another, too, "Do not celebrate, Deceived Orpheus...",[4] but assure you that I have nothing more on my conscience. I am not renouncing writing, but for a while, and even for a long while, I wish to stop publishing. Poetry is not a vain pleasure for me. I do not need their praises (I mean, of course, the crowd's), and do not see why I should subject myself to their abuses. I have read Nadeždin's criticism.[5] I do not know if I shall reply to it, or what I shall reply. He agrees with me in everything, only reproaches me for seeming to propose that elegance is not needed in elegant literature;[6] yet, as I said very clearly, I do not speak of the beautiful, because I shall be understood by few. The criticism has made me happy; it showed me that I achieved my aim completely – I convincingly refuted a common prejudice in everyone's sight – and that every reader who does a little thinking, seeing that the morality of literary works[7] is to be sought neither in choice of subject matter nor in sermons, nor this nor that, will conclude with me that it must be sought only in their truth, or in beauty, which is nothing but the highest truth. It would be a fine thing if I spoke Nadeždin's language. Among his thousand subscribers, I doubt if there is one who understood a word of the page on which he attempts to explain the beautiful. And what is most amusing of all is that there is a translation of it in the very foreword that he criticizes! If I reply, it will only be because I feel guilty in your eyes, having forced you to seek out and send me the journal for nothing. I am writing, but writing nothing decent. I am most dissatisfied with myself. "Not to lose time is to gain some," Voltaire used to say.[8] I console myself with that rule. I am now writing the life of Del'vig. That is only for you. You remind me of the Sverbeevs[9], whom, incidentally, I had not forgotten. Convey my regards to them, and tell them that if they stay in Moscow next winter I hope to pass many pleasant hours with them. I embrace you.

E. Baratynskij

[1] Taken from that same source, 26-27.

[2] Mar'ja Evgen'evna, born in the spring of 1832.
[3] Lit. 'with her enlightenment'.
[4] "Ne slav', obmanutyj Orfej", as Baratynskij calls it, appeared in *Severnye cvety* for 1832, 98, under the heading "Moj Elizij". As Orpheus joined Eurydice in the Elysian fields after his death, so Baratynskij will join Del'vig.
[5] "'Naložnica, sočinenie E. Baratynskogo", *Teleskop*, 1831, no. 10, 228-236.
[6] *Izjaščnaja literatura*, a fixed phrase meaning (effectively) any literature with literary pretensions, or accepted as such.
[7] Baratynskij judges poetry and prose by the same criterion — wholeness; see the introduction to the separate edition of "Naložnica" (*1951 edition*, 426-434) and "Antikritika", the reply to N. I. Nadeždin mentioned in the present letter as a future possibility (*ibid.*, 435-445). Art, Baratynskij claims, must be "many-sided"; only if it is not can it be morally harmful. Morality, that is to say, lies in wholeness of presentation. Thus only Homers and Shakespeares can, as perfect artists, be fully moral. Minor poets must complement each others' work. The polemics of 'morality in art' had been occasioned, in the 1820s, by Russian translations of novels by Balzac, Sue, Hugo and others of the curiously-named 'frenzied school', translations which Polevoj, among others, did all in his power to propagate.
[8] See note 3 to letter 28.
[9] Baratynskij was acquainted with D. N. Sverbeev and with his wife, Ekaterina Aleksandrovna, née Ščerbatova (1808-1892), from his first years in Moscow, 1825-1828. The Sverbeevs had a *salon* there. To Sverbeeva, Baratynskij dedicated a poem in 1829/30 ("K. A. Sverbeevoj", *Carskoe selo*, 1830, 133).

42

To I. V. Kireevskij   (29 October, 1831; Kajmary)[1]

There is even the date for you.[2] I missed one post because, in my perfect solitude,

> I forgot to call all the days
> Of the week by name.

I thought it was Monday when it was Wednesday. During that time, however, I was toiling for your periodical. I have replied to Nadeždin. My article is twice as large as my introduction, I think. I am amazed myself at writing so much prose. The fair copy of my drama is almost finished. Now I am working at a tale which you will remember: "The Ring".[3] All this you will receive by the next heavy post. It is all mediocre; but it will

[1] Taken from that same source, 28-29.
[2] It was not, unfortunately, Baratynskij's habit to place the date neatly in the top right-hand corner of his letters — probably because, as the letter suggests, he often did not know the exact date.
[3] "Persten'", a fantastic tale. The owner of the ring controls the fates. The tale was published by the obliging Kireevskij (*Evropeec*, 1832, Pt. 1, no. 2, 165-187).

do for a periodical. Thank you for your promise to send the Little Russian writer's tales.[4] As soon as I have read them I will write about them. I am somehow alarmed to write about Zagoskin. I am certainly not among his ardent admirers. His "Miloslavskij" is rubbish, and "Roslavlev" perhaps even worse.[5] The novel in "Roslavlev" is trivial; the historical approach is both stupid and uncertain. But how is one to tell these hard truths to an author who has all the same written the best novels we have? I am very sorry that Žukovskij does not like the title of my *poèma*.[6] I try to justify it in my reply to Nadeždin. I cannot understand why intelligent and enlightened people should be so outraged by a word the full sense of which is allowed in every conversation. Tell me what he thinks of the *poèma* itself, what he praises and what he condemns. Do not be afraid of making me sad. Žukovskij's opinion is particularly important to me, and his criticisms will be the more useful. I have a plan for a new *poèma*, and have considered it from all sides. Whether or not it will be good, God knows. I shall set to work in a day or two. I will not give you an account of the plan because that cools one's enthusiasm. The epistle to Jazykov, by the way, which you call European, is for *The European*. I will send you two or three more pieces by the next post. Farewell, convey my respects to your dear mother, to whom I shall not manage to write today. Remind Aleksej Andreevič[7] of me. How is his health, is his mind completely at rest on the score of cholera?

E. Baratynskij

My wife is on a pilgrimage to a nearby hermitage and will reply to your mother by the next post.

[4] *Večera na xutore bliz Dikan'ki*, by Gogol'. The first part came out in Moscow in in September 1831, and was rapturously received by Puškin. Gogol' was then a wandering figure, Professor of World History for a short, disastrous period in Petersburg University, author of the idyllic fiasco *Hans Küchel'garten*. Baratynskij recognized the merit of the "tales" immediately.

[5] M. N. Zagoskin's *Roslavlev*, despite Baratynskij's caustic comments, was a brilliant commercial success, selling 4,800 copies; see S. Gessen, *L'Editeur Alexandre Pouchkine* (Paris, 1930), 144. It rivaled that of Bulgarin's *Ivan Vyžigin*, which sold 2,000 copies in five days (March 26-31, 1829), so it is stated in *Severnaja pčela*, 1829, no. 40. By 1831, Polevoj's complaints of the miserable scale of Russian publishing were hardly justifiable (*Moskovskij telegraf*, 1828, 519-521). In that year, Polevoj had published — to support his argument — the following figures: in 1825, only 600 titles were published in the Russian Empire with a population of some 50 millions. Whereas in England, France and Germany, books were often printed in 10,000 or 20,000 copies, in Russia 1,200 was exceptional. Whereas in Russia only a few dozen journals and almanacs appeared, there were, in 1828, 490 in France, 483 in England, 840 in the USA, 150 in the Low Countries,

etc. The fact remains that in 1830 *Severnaja pčela* had a circulation of more than 3,000, and other periodicals did not lag far behind; see A. Meynieux, *op. cit.*, 471ff.
⁶ "Naložnica", or "Concubine".
⁷ A. A. Elagin, Kireevskij's father-in-law.

43

To I. V. Kireevskij   (December, 1831; Kajmary)¹

Here is something for *The European* for you. I am sorry that everything is so badly corrected: you know my passion for alterations. I could not hold myself back from them even on those poems that I am sending you. I am especially ashamed in the case of my drama, which did not merit them. Nor would I on any account have sent it to you, did I not think that in a journal even the mediocre is good to fill a few pages. Read through my reply to the critics,² and throw out what to you seems superfluous. I am very much afraid that I do not adhere to the German orthodoxy in it, and that a few heresies crept in. Print the drama without my name and read it to no one as my composition. Place the author's name under the tale.³ I have read your announcement: it could not have been written better, and I knew at once that it was yours. You commented on the journal's title both intelligently and modestly. But among us modesty is not understood, and I am afraid that there is not enough charlatanism in your announcement to gain subscribers. However, God's will... I shall subscribe to certain of the Russian periodicals next year and will stand up for you when necessary. Besides a plan for a *poèma*, I have sufficient bile in store; I shall be glad to give vent to it somehow. This letter is entirely a business letter. I must entrust you with a mission, not a literary one of course, but one not entirely divorced from literature either, for the subject in question is my stomach. I am sending you 50 roubles. Please do me the favour of having a half a pound of cocoa bought and send it to me by heavy post. It is sold on Hunter's Row: ask someone, perhaps even Èjnbrod,⁴ how to tell the fresh from the stale. Farewell, I embrace you heartily. Whatever else I write I will send. We are moving from the village into town. I will recommend *The European* to my Kazan' acquaintance.

E. Baratynskij

¹ Taken from that same source, 29-30.
² "Antikritika". Baratynskij took great trouble over his reply, which was skilfully drafted, and managed, in its last strophes, to throw Nadeždin with his own words.
³ "Persten'".
' Probably a store-keeper.

44

To I. V. Kireevskij   (Late December, 1831; Kazan')[1]

Thank you for your sensible criticism. In the end of my reply to Naděždin I warmed to my theme most inopportunely. Here is another version for you:
"The opening lines we willingly take for irony, consequently, as a careless joke at the expense of *The Moscow Telegraph's* disloyal captiousness. We shall not question the feeling of personal superiority that inspired them; we will merely note that they are inapposite and that they might be taken as an unguarded admission. We will allow the critic's fairness: in his partial analysis may be seen..." etc.

Change "a lack of logic" to "a lack of deliberation", and if any other expression should seem harsh to you, I entrust you to soften it.

The first number of your periodical is splendid. There can be no doubt of its success. It seems to me that we should bully the journalists, so that they divulge the existence of an opposition journal. Your announcement was too modest. Say if you have many subscribers. Print in the Moscow papers precisely what articles were placed in the 1st number of *The European*. That will be very useful to you.

I and my whole family sincerely wish you a most pleasant holiday and new year. God grant that we may be together in it.

We have moved from the village into town: I am harassed by boring visits. I shall get to know the society of this place, though not hoping to find any pleasure in it. There is nothing to be done: one must bow to custom, the more so because, in the main, custom is reasonable. I look upon myself as a traveller crossing tedious, monotonous steppes. Having crossed them, he will say "I saw them" with pleasure. Farewell, until next week.

                                        E. Baratynskij

Thank you for the cocoa. Probably the postage cost 15 roubles; if possible, send Žukovskij's new ballads by the next post.

[1]   Taken from that same source, 32-33. Dated on the basis of Baratynskij's sentence: "I and my whole family sincerely wish you a most pleasant holiday and new year."

Baratynskij's real interest in *Evropeec*, his dislike of society life and of its wearisome obligations, his constant wish to keep abreast of new literary events, are all emphasized again. The cost of postage was, relatively speaking, enormous. In 1834 he would sell 194 serfs for 37,000 roubles — at approximately 191 roubles per head. A serf was thus equal to six pounds of cocoa sent from Moscow (assuming that Kireevskij did buy half a pound, as asked).

45

To I. V. Kireevskij   (Early January, 1832; Kazan')[1]

I have just now received an unexpected and delightful novelty from you, the Guizot, which I very much wanted. Thank you. I notice that I have to repeat that phrase in each of my letters. Tell me if I owe you much: I have some money now.

I still do not know this town well. On my first day here I caught a heavy cold and could not go out. I may say, however, that in my opinion a provincial town is more animated than a capital. In saying "more animated" I do not mean 'more pleasant'; but here there is something missing in Moscow – activity. The conversations of some of our guests have been most entertaining to me. Each man speaks of his affairs or the affairs of the province, abuses or praises. Each man, so far as one can tell, is actively working for a positive aim, and therefore has some character. I cannot develop my thought for you fully, and will only say that in the provinces there is most certainly none of that indifference to everything that determines the character of most of our Moscow acquaintances. In the provinces there is more civic consciousness, more enthusiasm, there are more political and poetic elements. Observing this society more closely, perhaps I shall write something on it for your journal; but already I have seen enough to prefer a provincial town to a capital as a background for the action of a Russian novel. I praise your *European* here; but I do not know if my praises result in anyone's subscribing to it. Here only two or three families order books and journals,[2] and they then lend them to their acquaintances. The fearsome Arcybašev lives here.[3] I spoke with him, not knowing it was he. I shall try to get to know him better in order to examine his nature. When Kačenovskij was pointed out to me for the first time I looked at him with genuine curiosity, but my imagination had deceived me. I saw him, and there was nothing wild in his look.[4] I embrace you; embrace Jazykov for me. Best wishes to all your people.

---

[1]   Taken from that same source, 30-31.

[2]   It may well be that Baratynskij exaggerates the Kazan' population's indifference to *belles lettres* and pòetry in 1832; nevertheless his comment is most striking when one remembers that no Russian provincial town then had a greater population. According to Robert Pinkerton, esq. (*Russia, or Observations on the State*, etc., 2nd ed., London, 1833, 8), the population of Moscow was in 1833 approximately 250,000, of Petersburg 330,000, and of Kazan' a little more than 50,000. The virtual absence of interest in poetry in provincial towns was, of course, paralleled in the provinces of other countries

at a comparable stage of literary development. But in Russia, trade and commerce were already well developed by 1830, in which year imports totalled 192,000,000 roubles and exports 258,000,000 (*ibid.*, 15). On this trade, the government took 65,000,000 roubles in taxes. Members of the Russian merchant-manufacturing dynasties, of which Kazan' had representatives, were not poor in 1833 and might well have had pretensions to the culture that possession of a few issues of *Northern Flowers* or *The European* would indicate. Seemingly, those journals had a minute circulation or none at all outside the two great cities.

[3] Nikolaj Sergeevič Arcybašev (1773-1841), erstwhile opponent of Karamzin and the linguistic reforms of the period 1790-1805. The epithet is ironical; in 1832 Arcybašev was approaching sixty and no longer very fearsome.

[4] See note 3 to letter 28.

46

To I. V. Kireevskij   (January, 1832; Kazan')[1]

Thank you for your short letter, but do not be lazy, write the verbose one that you promised. You are greatly preoccupied with your journal now, I think, and have little time left for correspondence. I am slightly ashamed to force you to think about me, but you will forgive me for that. I, too, am not without worries, although of another kind. Provincial society life is rather wearisome, and now visiting, now receiving, I have little leisure left. Jazykov stirred me with his epistle.[2] It is delightful. Such serene grief, such gracious good nature! Such fresh sensitivity! By how much his blossoming muse excels all our pallid and sickly ones! Ours have hysteria, his has true inspiration! I have come to know Arcybašev. A very learned man and more decorous in conversation than in print, but completely sunk in his researches. Beyond a chronology of dates he sees nothing in history. The local *littérateurs* (you can imagine what *they* are like) intend to publish a journal and are asking me to participate in it. This is among the unpleasant aspects of my life here. Many people here have my works and Puškin's, but copied out, not printed. We must sell our editions a little cheaper.[3] I am sending *The Telescope* off to you. Farewell, I am hurrying to send this to the post where, I hope, a parcel is waiting for me from you, containing *The European*.

[1] Taken from that same source, 33-34.

[2] "I. V. Kireevskomu (v al'bom)", or "Poèt, vxožu ja gordelivo...", written on November 21, 1831, was not published until 1886 (*Russkaja starina*, no. 7, 171).

[3] A copy of *Naložnica: sočinenie E. Baratynskogo*, printed by Avgust Semen (1831), cost ten roubles in the year of its publication.

47

To I. V. Kireevskij   (18 January, 1832; Kazan')[1]

I have had no letters from you for a long time, dear Kireevskij, and am
not complaining, for I know that you have plenty to occupy you. I have a
request to make of you: if my first epistle to Jazykov has not yet been
printed, do not print it: it seems to me rather weak.[2] Print the second,
rather,[3] with which I am more satisfied. I am leading the most stupid life
here, dissipated but affording no pleasure, and can scarcely wait for our
return to the country. We are moving in the first week of Lent.[4] There I
hope to employ my time usefully for myself and for *The European*, but
here there is simply no possibility of it. Imagine whom I found in Kazan'!
Young Percov,[5] celebrated for his jokes in rhyme, which Puškin praised to
us; but he is not only a highly intelligent man – he is also a highly
educated one, and with decided talent. He read me extracts from his
comedy in verse which is full of liveliness and wit. I will try to get them
from him for *The European*. Only with him do I speak my natural language here. There you have a report on my way of life. Why do you not
send me *The European*? I have received Žukovskij's ballads.[6] There is a
remarkable perfection of style in some, and simplicity, which Žukovskij
did not have in his earlier works. He even makes me want to put legends
to rhyme. Farewell, I embrace you.

E. Baratynskij

---

[1]   Taken from that same source, 31-32.
[2]   "N. M. Jazykovu" ("Jazykov, bujstva molodogo..."), was published, in spite of its
author's protestations, in *Evropeec*, 1832, no. 2, 204. Baratynskij sent a copy of the
epistle to Jazykov himself, together with the note:" Here are a few clumsy rhymes for
you, dear Jazykov, which, however, show how I think of you." Jazykov wrote on the
bottom of the letter: "Received 1831, November 23"; see *Istoriko-literaturnyj sbornik,
posvjaščennyj V. I. Sreznevskomu* (Leningrad, 1924), 13-14. Baratynskij met Jazykov
at the Kireevskijs', through the good offices of Kireevskij's in-laws, the Elagins.
[3]   "Jazykovu" ("Byvalo, svet pozabyvaja..."), first published in the verse collection of
1835, 47. This second epistle was received by the addressee on January 14, 1832 — less
than three months after the first; the second epistle was published after some delay, for
reasons that are unclear. It was inspired by Jazykov's own epistle to I. V. Kireevskij
(see note 2 to letter 46). On sending his second offering, which was written somewhat in
Jazykov's own style, Baratynskij added: "Here is what your epistle inspired in me, your
epistle full of freshness and beauty and sadness and rapture (*vostorg*)... Your student
elegies will live on to posterity, but you are right in wishing to select a new path..."; see
Literaturno-bibliologičeskij sbornik (Petrograd, 1918), 70. (Jazykov spoke, in his
epistle to Kireevskij, of dealing with "Russian antiquity".)
[4]   Lit. 'Great, or Easter, Fast'; the move would therefore probably occur in March.
In fact the family did not leave Kazan' until the last days of June; see letter 54.
[5]   Erast Petrovič Percov (1804-1873), a minor poet and dramatist whom Baratynskij

overrated. Percov was not in Kazan' entirely by chance; the family was established in the province of Kazan'. Petr Petrovič Percov (1868-1947), publisher and literary critic, studied law at Kazan' University and maintained his connections in that city.

[6] *Ballady i povesti V. Žukovskogo* (St.P., 1831). Baratynskij had already leaned in the direction of 'rhyming legends' in "Besenok", published in *Svernye cvety* for 1829, 187; and in that poem there had been mention of Gromoboj, hero of Žukovskij's celebrated ballad "Dvenadcat' spjaščix dev".

48

To I. V. Kireevskij   (February, 1832; Kazan')[1]

I understand that the journalist's troubled life and especially its dissonant rumours and gossip should agitate you in an unpleasant way, brother Kireevskij. I foresaw your position and am sorry that I am not with you, because we view life in a similar way and have strengthened one another in that view. Žukovskij's, Puškin's and Vjazemskij's opinion seems to me unjust. We shall not move the public by accommodating ourselves to it. Writers teach the public, and if the public finds something incomprehensible in them, that inspires still more respect for knowledge it does not have, forcing it to search for that knowledge and even to be ashamed of its own ignorance. Polevoj, I would hope, is less clear than you,[2] but still his journal has sold out and is, no doubt, doing a great service, for if it does not give one ideas, it stimulates them; but you both provide ideas *and* stimulate them. Everyone has a right to abuse the public, and the public never grows angry at this, for what is said of a collective body none of its members takes as directed at himself. Vjazemskij made a witticism, that is all. If you have few subscribers, the reasons are (1) the over-modest announcement, (2) your lack of fame as a writer, (3) the whims of fashion.[3] But have patience and publish again next year, and I will guarantee its success. We subscribed to *The European* on reading the first number here in Kazan'. In general, the journal has been well received. It is found intelligent, learned, and varied. Believe me, Russians have a special ability and a special need to reflect. Give them something to bite on and they will thank you. Do not forget, however, that it must have a mixed character, and tales, without which the journal will not be a journal but a

[1] Taken from that same source, 36-37.
[2] N. A. Polevoj's *Moskovskij telegraf* was a rival in the same journalistic field that *Evropeec* entered — and so quickly left.
[3] Lit. 'the exception(s) of fashion(s)'.

book.[4] Your article on the nineteenth century[5] is incomprehensible to the public only in that part where you deal with philosophy and, indeed, your conclusions are intelligible only to those initiated in the mysteries of the latest metaphysic; conversely, the literary inferences and application of this same philosophy to reality, are quite clear through a *feeling* of knowing that philosophy, which is not yet wholly intelligible to the mind. I do not know if you will understand me; but such is man's way of thinking that we believe before investigating or, rather, we only investigate to prove to ourselves that we were right in our convictions. This is why I find it useful to act as you do, that is, to acquaint your readers with the results of science in order, having forced them to admire it, to oblige them to concern themselves with it. I am trying to send you something for no. 3. You are right, Kazan' has not been very stimulating for me. I hope, however, that some of the impressions and observations that I have gathered will not be wasted. Farewell, do not lose heart. Literary work is its own reward; among us, thank God, the degree of respect that we attain, as writers, is not in proportion to our commercial success. That I know for sure and by experience. Despite his success in that direction, Bulgarin is despised even in the provinces; I have not yet met the people for whom he writes.

E. Baratynskij

[4] Baratynskij seems to have been faintly aware, but aware nevertheless, of the necessity of including at least a fashion section, if not a political section, in any journal that aspired to a wide circulation in the fourth decade. Writing to Vjazemskij in mid-October 1831 (*A. S. Puškin, 1962*, vol. 10, 73), Puškin at once enquired (of *The European*) "will there be fashions in it?" No later than September 3 he had declared, also to Vjazemskij (*ibid.*, vol. 10, 66-67), "There's no use thinking of a political newspaper, but we might try a monthly or four-monthly neutral journal. There is one rub: *without fashions* it won't sell, and *with fashions* for us to take a position alongside Šalikov, Polevoj etc., would be shameful." Vjazemskij, shrewd as usual, ridiculed Puškin's suggestion that a fashion section should appear once every four months, noting that fashions change every fourth day.

[5] "Devjatnadcatyj vek", published in the opening no. of *Evropeec*.

49

To I. V. Kireevskij (22 February, 1832; Kazan')[1]

I am beginning my letter with reproaches, and I have gathered a collection of them. First, you do not write if I owe you much for the Guizot and

[1] Taken from that same source, 37-38.

other trifles. No, there is no being civil with you, especially in that. Second, allow me to have words with you for not giving me your opinion of my drama. Probably you do not care for it; but is it possible that you know me so little as to fear offending my author's pride by telling me openly that I have written rubbish? I shall be the happier for your praises when I see you are not humoring me. I have received the second booklet of *The European*. The review of "The Concubine" was a real service to me. It is a pity that little is written among us, especially anything good, or you would make a name for yourself with your literary reviews. You understand me completely, entered the poet's soul and grasped the poetry that I dream when I write. Your phrase: *carries us into a musical and dreamily-expansive atmosphere* made me start with joy, for that very quality I suspected in myself in moments of pride as a writer, but expressed it worse. It is impossible for me not to believe in your sincerity: without conviction there is no poetry, and your phrase is that of a poet. I am not in the least angry that you condemn the genre I chose. I think the same about it myself, and wish to abandon it. In general the second booklet of *The European* is not inferior to the first. We are moving from the town into the country. I hope that I shall write, at least, I have the firm intention not to indulge my laziness. If verses prove obstinate I shall take up prose. Farewell, I embrace you.

E. Baratynskij

I have received the cocoa.

50

To I. V. Kireevskij   (14 March, 1832; Kazan')[1]

I have attributed your silence to lack of time and have not imagined anything unpleasant; you may imagine how I was affected by your letter in which you tell me of so many domestic cares and, finally, of the closure of your journal.[2] Your mother's illness (and it is not the first

---

[1]   Taken from that same source, 40-41.
[2]   As a direct result of Kireevskij's article "Devjatnadcatyj vek", and an indirect consequence of the journal's liberal stance, *Evropeec* was banned on February 22, 1832. Baratynskij was deeply distressed, and kept his promise, given in the conclusion of this letter, to write but not to publish. In 1833-1834, indeed, he published a mere two

since we parted) has deeply grieved us, despite the fact that, according to your letter, she is improved. I cannot recover from the suppression ot your journal. There is no doubt that it is the work of an unjust secret and despicable informer, but what comfort is there in that? After this, what can one undertake in literature? How is one to bring him to court? Together with you, I have lost a strong incentive to engage in literary work. The suppression of your journal simply brought the spleen on me, and judging by your letter it has produced a state of melancholy in you. What is to be done? We will reflect in silence, and leave the literary arena to the Polevojs and Bulgarins. Let us thank providence for having made us friends, that each of us found in the other a man who understands him, and that there are still a few who are sympathetic to us both in heart and in mind. We will shut ourselves in our circle, like the first Christian brotherhoods, inheritors of the earth,[3] driven out in their time but now triumphant. We will write, but not publish. Perhaps a happier time may come. Farewell, my dear friend, I embrace you. Write to me. I need your letters. You will find that persuasion a strong one.

E. Baratynskij

My wife earnestly requests you to tell us about your mother's recovery.

---

poems — "Na smert' Gete" and "Kol'co", both given to *Novosel'e*. Success, among a wide public, depends on publication; there is no surer sign of the neglect of any public, wide or narrow, than not to publish at all. Nor is it feasible that Baratynskij's unwonted silence was occasioned by his wish to produce the greater impact with his verse collection of 1835. That collection was announced in nos. 32 and 35 of *Moskovskie vedomosti* for 1835; but publication had been planned for 1832 or 1833. In a letter to P. V. Naščokin of December 2, 1832, Puškin informed him that he had discussed the edition with Smirdin, and was thinking in terms of ten thousand copies; *A. S. Puškin, 1962*, vol. 10, 116. The censors had given clearance to the collection by March of 1833. Puškin notes the banning of the journal in a letter to I. I. Dmitriev of February 14, 1832: "Probably you already know that the journal *The European* has been suppressed in consequence of a denunciation. Kireevskij, kind and shy Kireevskij, has been represented to the government as a madcap and a Jacobin! Everyone here hopes he will succeed in justifying himself and that the slanderers — or the slander, at least — will be abashed and unmasked." It was Nicholas himself, in fact, who had 'discovered' political allusions hostile to himself in two articles by Kireevskij. The fate of the latter's journal was sealed when, under police interrogation, he openly remarked that the serfs should certainly be liberated.

[3]   Lit. 'holders of the earth'. The biblical allusion, however, is obvious.

51

To I. V. Kireevskij   (April-May, 1832; Kazan')[1]

I have not written to you for so long that I am truly ashamed. I have been silent not out of laziness, nor because I had no time, but simply because. This *because* is the Russian absolute, but to explain it is impossible. Today I have no time to write letters properly speaking, because I am writing verse, yet here I am sitting over a manuscript for you! How can this be, if not because? I am most grateful to Janovskij[2] for his present. I would very much like to meet him. Never before have we had an author with such cheerful cheerfulness, it is a great rarity among us in the north. Janovskij is a man of decided talent. His style is lively, original, filled with colour and, often, with taste. The observer in him is plain in many passages, and he is more than once a poet in his tale "A Terrible Vengeance". Our numbers have increased: this conclusion is a little immodest, but it reflects my feeling towards Janovskij well.

Of Xomjakov's tragedy[3] you wrote to me only that it is finished. Tell me about it in more detail. My brother,[4] to whom Xomjakov read it, writes to me from Petersburg that it excels Puškin's "Boris" by far, but says nothing from which one might form an impression of it. I am relying on you for that.

Thank kind Karolina[5] for me for her translation of "The Transmigration of Souls". Never have I been more vexed that I do not know German. I am sure that she has translated me splendidly, and it would be more amusing for me to read myself in her translation than in the original: just as you recognize yourself more willingly in a somewhat flattering portrait than in the mirror.

My sister Sonečka[6] is not angry with you for suspecting a little coquetry in Gorskina.[7] The point is not in your suspicion, however, but in the fact that she has heard rumours that you see a great similarity between them, from which it follows that you hold the same opinion of her; but she will not admit its justness.

Farewell, dear friend; do me the goodness of writing and telling me your rank: I need to know it in order to write you a receipt on the Council of Trustees. That will give you no trouble: they will deliver it to you, and

[1] Taken from that same source, 44-45.
[2] Gogol' sent Baratynskij a copy of his *Večera na Xutore bliz Dikan'ki* in Kazan'. The second part of the work appeared in March, 1832.
[3] *Dmitrij Samozvanec.* Aleksej Stepanovič Xomjakov (1804-1860) was a worthy leader of the Slavophile party in the middle decades of the century. His political verse, such

that is all. How are the Sverbeevs? Convey my regards to them, as to all your people.

Your Baratynskij

Write to me quickly about your rank. I am leaving here on May 25.

---

as that inspired by the disastrous Crimean War, is dignified and, sometimes, grand. Baratynskij seems to have been unaware that Xomjakov was more than a soldier-writer, or promising dramatist. He was, in reality, one of the greatest of all lay theologians and a distinguished philosopher of history. Xomjakov saw man's freedom as attainable only through membership of a greater body, or union — the Christian Church. Russia, although unworthy, was to redeem the West from the shackles of materialism, individualism, and its accompanying pride.

Dmitrij Samozvanec, written in 1831, was published in the early spring of 1833. Baratynskij's later opinion of the work was shared by Puškin. "I have hopes for Xomjakov," he informed Jazykov on November 18, 1831; "his *Pretender* will no longer be a student, but his verses will continue excellent as before". (Puškin trusted that Xomjakov had outgrown the deficiencies of *Ermak*, which was written as a 'student' of literature.)

[4] Iraklij, then an inhabitant of Petersburg.

[5] Karolina Janiš (Jaenisch) (1807-1893), better known as Karolina Pavlova, translated a number of Baratynskij's elegies into German in 1833 (*Das Nordlicht. Proben der neueren russischen Litteratur von Karoline Jaenisch*, Dresden and Leipzig). Karolina Pavlova selected pieces by Puškin, Del'vig, Jazykov and Venevitinov, as well as by Baratynskij, and repeated her efforts in 1839 for a French public (*Les Préludes*, Paris). On the translations, see I. V. Kireevskij, *Sobranie sočinenij v dvux tomax*, vol. 2 (Moscow, 1911), 593; also comments by N. M. Gajdenkov in the *Sovetskij Pisatel'* edition of Pavlova's verse, *Polnoe sobranie stixotvorenij* (Leningrad, 1964). Baratynskij had earlier made considerable efforts to acquire a knowledge of German and had, he informed his mother in 1824, tormented the officers at Gel'singfors who knew the language; see *1884 edition*, 498. Application, however, seems to have proved insufficient.

[6] Sophie Èngel'gardt (1811-1884), the wife of N. V. Putjata.

[7] An unknown woman.

52

To I. V. Kireevskij   (30 May, 1832; Kazan')[1]

My father-in-law[2] has arrived in Moscow. I was to have gone down to Tambov to my mother's at one time, where I intended to pass the summer, but my wife's illness held me back. Write to me in Kazan' as before. I cannot imagine what kind of tragedy Xomjakov's is. Dmitrij the Pretender is a wholly historical character; willy-nilly, our imagination gives him a

[1] Taken from that same source, 46.

[2] Lev Nikolaevič Èngel'gardt; see note 6 to letter 25.

physiognomy in keeping with the accounts of chroniclers.To idealize him would be the summit of art. Byron's Sardanapulus[3] is a misty character, to whom the poet could give such expression as he chose. There was no one to say: he's not like that. But it is as though we had all seen Dmitrij and we judge the poet as we judge a portrait-painter. The genre chosen by Xomjakov is extremely attractive: it offers a wide frame for poetry. But it seems to me that it is better suited to Ermak[4] than to Dmitrij. Will he publish his tragedy soon? I am most impatient to read it, the more so since its publication will contradict all my notions, and I hope to draw completely new poetical impressions from it.[5] All I have written recently has been small pieces. I have five of them now, including one, on the death of Goethe, with which I am more satisfied than with the others.[6] I am not sending you all these so as to have something to read when we meet. Forgive me for that Xvostovish sentiment.[7] Farewell. My family will spend three days in Moscow.[8] See them once or twice: they will tell you about our adventures in Kazan'.

[3] Eponymous hero of *Sardanapulus: a Tragedy* (1821).
[4] The Cossack leader Ermak was, like Suvorov, Ermolov and other Russian leaders, treated as a hero by the Russian civic poets, notably Ryleev, A. A. Bestužev and Kjuxel'beker. For these men, poetry "was the means of life's ideal transformation" (A. G. Cejtlin, *Tvorčestvo Ryleeva*, Moscow, 1955, 233), and a means by which the populace might be prepared for carefully undefined future action (against autocracy). Such, in Ryleev's own words, was the chief aim of his *Dumy* (1824) (*ibid.*, 99). Again, according to the *zakonopoloženie* of the Union of Welfare (see *Dekabristy: otryvki iz istočnikov*, ed., Ju. G. Oksman, Moscow, 1926, 84-101), members of that society were, inspired "by love of the commonweal", to spread abroad a love of good, a consciousness of civic duty and a feeling of "high patriotism". History was, of course, capable of interpretation — and interpreted. Those who best embodied the idea of patriotism became heroes of the liberal cause. As a counter-measure against the proselyting and expansive policy of Kuchum, the last khan of the Siberian Tatars, the Stroganovs took into their service a Cossack soldier of fortune, Ermak, and a band of his men. He was equipped to forage for booty and tribute east of the Urals, and, armed with gunpowder, won a series of victories between 1581 and 1585, when he was besieged and drowned. Such was 'the conquest of Siberia'.
[5] 'Impressions' is a Gallicism. Baratynskij means, one imagines, 'new ideas'.
[6] "Na smert' Gete". Goethe died on March 22, 1832, and the poem was completed by late May, possibly even earlier. In Goethe, Baratynskij saw the perfect artist. In him, "flaming imagination and cold intellect" met (see "Tavrida", *1951 edition*, 425). Opposite poles of thought and feeling produced, in Baratynskij's conceit of the German (whose work he could not read in original), the synthesis of genius. Already in 1819, A. I. Turgenev had written an ecstatic "K portretu Gete". The universality of Goethe's work and his Olympian independence, which attracted Turgenev, attracted Baratynskij also. Goethe was a scientist and prophet, poet and Minister of State — above all, a man in whom there was 'wholeness' that eluded Baratynskij and his work.
[7] An allusion to Count D. I. Xvostov (1757-1835), a third-rate poet mocked by Puškin (*A. S. Puškin, 1962*, vol. 9, 48, 133, 164, 213, 286), and by others of his circle.
[8] A. F. Baratynskaja owned a house in Moscow.

53

To I. V. Kireevskij　　　　　　　　　　　　(June, 1832; Kazan')[1]

You developed your idea about the fable for me with striking clarity. I wish you would write an article on it. Your idea is new and, I am convinced, just: it is worth an article. I am keeping your letters, and when we meet in Moscow I will search out those two in which you speak about the fable. You will put what you said in them into your article, for it would be hard to express oneself better. You are an uncommon critic, and the suppression of *The European* is a great loss for you. Is it possible that you have written nothing since then? How is your novel? Weiland,[2] I think, said that if he lived on an uninhabited island he would polish his verses with as much care as if he were in a circle of *littérateurs*. You must prove to us that Weiland was speaking from the heart. For us, Russia *is* uninhabited, and our disinterested labour will demonstrate the lofty morality of our thought. I have read "Car' Saltan" here.[3] It is a perfect Russian tale, and in this, it seems to me, is its shortcoming. What kind of poetry is it to put Eruslan Lazarevič or the Fire-Bird to rhyme, word by word? And what does that add to our literary heritage? Let us leave the materials of folk-poetry in their original form, or gather them into a complete whole which would excel them by as much as a good story excels contemporary memoirs. Poetic materials cannot be gathered into a complete whole otherwise than by a poetical plan that accords with their spirit and which, as far as possible, embraces them all. Puškin certainly does not have this. His tale is equal in merit to one of our ancient tales – and that is all. One can even say that his is not the best among them. How far it is from this imitation of Russian tales to Del'vig's imitation of Russian songs! In a word, Puškin's tale did not satisfy me at all. Farewell, greet Sverbeev and his wife from me. Write to me as before, in Kazan'. I do not know if I shall be here a long time. I shall try to be in Moscow in July in order to see Žukovskij and to embrace you sooner, but I do not know yet if it will be possible.

---

[1]　Taken from *Tatevskij sbornik S. A. Račinskogo* (St.P., 1899), 48-49. Dated June, since Baratynskij had not yet left Kazan'.
[2]　Christopher-Martin Weiland (1733-1813), German writer; see V. I. Kulešov, *op. cit.*, 28, 38, 62, 89.
[3]　Puškin's "Skazka o care Saltane" appeared in *Stixotvorenija Aleksandra Puškina* (St.P., March 1832).

54

To I. V. Kireevskij   (20 June, 1832; Kazan')[1]

I am writing to you from Kazan' for the last time. On the 19th I am leaving for Tambov. Address your letters to me now: Tambov Province, town of Kirsanov. What you say about Hugo and Barbier[2] makes me feel still more impatient to return to Moscow, if that is possible. There have proved insufficient new heartfelt convictions, insufficient enlightened fanaticism, to create a new poetry: enlightened fanaticism, as I see it, is what has appeared with Barbier. But it is not likely that he will find a response in us. We are so far from the arena of recent events that we understand it very imperfectly, and feel it still less. We look on the European enthusiasts almost as the sober watch the drunk, and if their transports are sometimes comprehensible to our *mind*, they practically never captivate our heart.[3] What is for them reality is for us abstraction. Only individualistic poetry is natural to us. Egoism is our established deity, for we have thrown away the old idols and not yet come to believe in new ones.[4] A person who finds nothing to worship outside himself must become absorbed in himself. That is our role for the present. Perhaps we shall take it into our heads to imitate Barbier, but there will be nothing alive in those systematic attempts, and the nature of things[5] will turn us onto a road more natural for us. Farewell, give my regards to your people. One day I shall ask you to rent yourself a house in Moscow! One day I shall sit with you from eight in the evening until three or four in the morning, dreaming philosophic dreams and not noticing how time flies! Once in Moscow, I hope not to part from you for a long time, but to give my life the settled habits that I have long wished for.

[1]   Taken from that same source, 47-48. The date is not certain; June 20 is written in *Tatevskij sbornik S. A. Račinskogo*. In the letter, however, he informs Kireevskij of his intention to leave, as it were, yesterday. Baratynskij may have dated the letter as an afterthought, and made the error; or there may have been no date on the original, which is lost, and the error may have originated in 1899.

[2]   Victor Hugo (1802-1885) and Henri-August Barbier (1805-1882) became popular in Russia after the Decembrist rising. N. A. Polevoj published an enthusiastic "O romanax V. Gjugo" in *Moskovskij telegraf*, 1832, Pt. 43, nos. 17 and 18. A collection of verse by Barbier entitled *Les Jambes*, published immediately after the July Revolution, was translated within nine months (*Jamby*, 1832). By June of that year, Baratynskij was conscious of the fact that others were discussing the collection — and that he, living in Kazan', had no copy and could not buy one.

[3]   Here Baratynskij speaks for himself, not for Kireevskij's or Polevoj's generations.

[4]   By "old idols", the rules and conventions of neo-classicism are presumably meant. The 'new idols' are Hugo, Balzac, Barbier, Sue *et al.*

[5]   Lit. 'the strength of things...'.

55

To P. A. Vjazemskij   (December, 1832; Moscow)[1]

My brother[2] will deliver this letter to you, dear prince, and I ask you to receive him kindly. Literary connections are sometimes of as much value as blood relationships, and I entrust him to you fully believing this.

I have been long in replying to your kind, friendly letter, but I am deeply grateful to you for it.

Moscow misses you.[3] There is not a company in which you are not remembered and where your absence has not been complained of. I have made the acquaintance of your old friend M. Orlov[4] and his most amiable wife. Among the circle which you once frequented your moving away is felt still more. D. Davydov sent me the beginning of your epistle to him[5] in which you imitate his style poetically. He is thinking of galloping to Moscow for a couple of weeks. Won't you decide to follow his example and invite Puškin to come with you? Then the word will be deed, then

> All the fellows in the friendly artel'
> Will be present.[6]

I am writing nothing new and consort with the past. I have sold Smirdin[7] a complete collection of my verses. It seems that it will certainly be the last and I shall add nothing to it. The time of individualistic poetry has passed, another has not yet ripened.

Convey my respects to the princess and be assured of my lasting devotion towards yourself.

---

[1] Taken from the original, preserved in the Baratynskij Archive, *CGALI*. Dated on the basis of the reference to A. Smirdin; see *A. S. Puškin, 1962*, vol. 10, 116. Puškin discussed the publication of the eventual collection of 1835 with Smirdin on December 2, 1832 (and was thinking of 8,000 or 10,000 copies — more than Baratynskij might at first agree to).

[2] Iraklij Abramovič; see note 2 to letter 3.

[3] Vjazemskij had abandoned Moscow for Petersburg.

[4] Mixail Fedorovič Orlov (1788-1842), General-Major and a veteran of the Napoleonic Wars, was much respected in post-Decembrist Moscow and Petersburg for the part he had played in the ill-fated Liberal movement. Orlov had been a member of the Society of Arzamas, and active in the Union of Welfare (suggesting, at a meeting in January 1821, that the Union publish anti-government literature and mint and disseminate counterfeit currency, thus bringing the government into discredit; see A. G. Mazour, *op. cit.*, 81-82). It is some measure of the injustice of the 'trial' of the Decembrists, and of the ineptitude of the Special Supreme Court established by Nicholas, that

Orlov was freed. Morally he was as guilty as anyone for the conspiracy. Ten years after the event, "he paced the floor" of various Moscow *salons* "like a lion in a cage ... hungry for action" (Herzen, *Byloe i dumy*, Pt. 1, Chap. 8). Orlov's "most amiable wife" was also of strong Liberal antecedents — Ekaterina Nikolaevna Raevskaja (1805-1885).

[5] "K staromu gusaru" (1832), written on the occasion of Davydov's verse collection appearing in that year.

The *artel'* referred to is the friends who gathered in Vjazemskij's Moscow house in 1810-1811: Denis Vasil'evič Davydov himself, Fedor Tolstoj, Žukovskij, Vasilij Puškin and Batjuškov.

[6] A paraphrase of 11. 49-50 of Vjazemskij's poem.

[7] The deal was later cancelled; *Sumerki*, Baratynskij's last verse collection (1842), was printed by Semen.

56

To I. V. Kireevskij   (15 October, 1833; Mara)[1]

I thank you sincerely for your gift. I have received your portrait. It is a good likeness, even a very good one; but like all portraits and all transla-tions – unsatisfactory. It is strange that painters who occupy themselves exclusively with portraits cannot catch, during a conversation, the true, fleeting expression of the original, but copy only the client. I remember Berger's[2] soulless system, which he himself explained to me. In his view, the portrait-painter should not give rein to his imagination, should not interpret the face that he has copied as he fancies, but accurately follow all the physical lines and entrust the likeness to that precision. Even here he was true to his system, so your portrait may delight all those who do not know you as intimately as I, but it leaves me highly satisfied with the parcel and dissatisfied with the artist. About myself I have almost nothing to tell you. I am wallowing in money calculations. Small wonder: we have a real famine. We must buy 2,000 quarters of rye as provisions for the peasants.[3] That, at the present prices, will cost 40,000. Such circumstances can make one stop and think. And it is on me, as the eldest of the family, that responsibility for active measures lies. Farewell, I send my warmest respects to all your family.

E. Baratynskij

[1] Taken from *Tatevskij sbornik S. A. Račinskogo* (St.P., 1899), 50-51.
[2] Philippe Berger (1783-1867) came to Petersburg to try his fortune in 1823. He produced an unexciting aquarelle of Baratynskij, which is reproduced in the *Academy edition*, vol. 1, 120/21.
[3] This letter somewhat redeems a harsh letter written from Tambov province in 1830 (*Tatevskij arxiv*, 25), in which the poet describes the effects of famine in the

township of Ržev: "La disette y a produit une véritable insurrection ... plus de trois milles personnes ont quitté le district — tous serfs. Les déménagements ne se font pas sans violence. Ils commencent par s'emparer de tout ce qu'ils peuvent trouver dans les maisons de leur maîtres ... c'est une mauvais plaisanterie." Security, not peasant suffering, is the main concern here.

57

To I. V. Kireevskij   (28 November, 1833; Mara)[1]

The other day I received from Smirdin the programme for his journal, together with a letter inviting me to collaborate. I do not know if he will be successful in this speculation.[2] There is no comparing the French writers with ours; but there is nothing weaker or paler than Ladvocat's "One Hundred and One".[3] All the same, we must help him. His courage and energy deserve all our approval. Are you preparing something for him? Do you know that you have a fine article ready for a journal? That is on the theory of dress, which could be published in extract. I remembered it recently, on reading Balzac's theory of the gait.[4] Comparing the two articles, I found that there is a good deal of similarity between you in turn of mind and even in style, but with this difference, that you still have a wide field before you, and can avoid his shortcomings. You have now what he had originally: conscientious refinement of expression. He, noticing its effectiveness, became less conscientious and even more refined. You are conscientious still, and will avoid his stiffness. You, like him, have a need to generalize ideas, the desire to show that every object and every fact is in sympathy and conformity with the whole world system; but he, it seems to me, is guilty of excessive bragging of his

---

[1] Taken from that same source, 51-52.

[2] In 1834, Smirdin together with Osip-Julian Ivanovič Senkovskij (1800-1858), belletriste, journalist and Professor of Oriental Languages at Petersburg University (Senkovskij was an Arabist), published *Biblioteka dlja čtenija*. Baratynskij need not have worried on the journal's account; Smirdin was a shrewd speculator and the journal survived until 1865, under the editorship of K. A. Polevoj (1834-1841), M. D. Ol'xin (1841-1848) and P. D. Boborykin (1848-1865). It followed no particular literary direction or school, but was mildly sympathetic towards anything the popularity of which had been elsewhere proved already.

[3] A reference to *Le livre des cent et un* by Charles Ladvocat (1790-1854),347.

[4] "Théorie de la Démarche", one of a series of 'analytic essays' written between 1830 and 1833 ("Physiologie des positions", "— de la toilette", "— du cigare", etc.,) appeared in *L'Europe Littéraire*, Aug. 15, 18, 25 and Sept. 5, 1833. Within three months, possibly two (since Baratynskij read the piece "not long ago"), copies of the journal had made their way from Paris to Tambov.

learning, and of the theatrical adoption of the technical jargon of every science. Success has rather spoiled him. Nor do I like his over-general, too thoughtless sentimentalism. His constant pretensions to profound thinking do not wholly conceal his French empty-headedness. How can a thinker admit that he has not embraced a single conviction? And is it not even more laughable to boast of that? *You* may be a Balzac with two or three opinions (which will give you a foothold that he lacks), with a more direct and rapid style, but just as distinct a one. Farewell, my respects to your people.

E. Baratynskij

Do me a favour: find out Puškin's country and town addresses; I must write to him. I am unsealing the letter deliberately to ask this.

58

To I. V. Kireevskij (4 December, 1833; Mara)[1]

You sadden me with your bad news. How are your eyes? I hope this letter will find you sighted.[2] I have had occasion to praise solitude, but not the sort that blindness brings. About solitude, by the way. You raise the question again as to which is preferable, society life or the secluded life. The one and the other are necessary to our development. One must receive impressions, and one must sum them up. So, too, sleep and waking, food and digestion are necessary. It remains to define in what proportion the one shall be to the other. That depends on each man's temperament. As far as I am concerned, I say about society what Famusov[3] says about dinners:

You eat for three hours, and can't digest it in three days.

You belong to the new generation,[4] which thirsts for excitement, I – to

[1] Taken from that same source, 52-53.
[2] I. V. Kireevskij's sight was weak. A sketch by Dmitriev-Mamonov, reproduced in *A. S. Puškin, 1962*, vol. 10, 48/49, shows him wearing spectacles.
[3] An undesirable character in *Gore ot uma* (1822-1824), a brilliant four-act comedy in freely rhymed iambics by Aleksandr Sergeevič Griboedov (1794-1829). The quoted line is from Act 2, scene 1, 12.
[4] That is, the German-orientated generation. Kireevskij justly noted in "Obozrenie russkoj slovesnosti za 1829 god" that "there entered two elements into our literature: the French and German ways of thought". (He might have said "entered our cultural

the old, which prayed to God to spare them from it. You call ardent activity happiness; I am scared by it, and see happiness rather in peace. Each of us drew these opinions from his age. But this is not merely a matter of opinions, but also of feelings. Our sensibilities were formed in accordance with the concepts with which our minds were fed. Even though each of us adopted the theoretic system of another, still we should not change in essence. Our emotional needs would remain the same. By solitude I do not mean isolation; I mean

> A refuge from the visitations of society,
> Barred by a reliable door,
> But with a grateful heart open
> To friendship and the maidens of inspiration.[5]

I shall build myself such a refuge sooner or later, and hope that you will visit me in it. I embrace you.

E. Baratynskij

---

life...".) Kireevskij was born in 1806, and six years' age difference was vital in that time. Still in 1841, S. P. Ševyrev could declare that "one may justly divide all educated Russians into two camps: the French and the German, according to the influence of one or other education" ("Vzgljad russkogo na sovremennoe obrazovanie Evropy", *Moskvitjanin*, 1841, Pt. 1, 246). Baratynskij perhaps overemphasizes his own antiquity; but the difference in cultural outlook was indisputable.

[5] Possibly a draft for "Vot vernyj spisok vpečatlenij..." (see *1957 edition*, 215-216), which Baratynskij intended to use as an introduction to the collection of 1835 but did not.

59

To I. V. Kireevskij   (Spring, 1834; Mara)[1]

I am to blame for not having written to you for so long, dear Kireevskij. The reason is, first, the headaches to which I am prone, and which have visited me two postal days running as though on purpose; then, I live with such worries and find myself affected by such feelings (I briefly mentioned to you in how poor a condition my mother's health is), that I have not always the strength to take up the pen. Am *I* to propose topics for literary articles to *you*? I long ago lost sight of general questions for the sake of a private life.[2] But might I not propose to you, for example, the very subject of which I am speaking: social life and private life? How

[1] Taken from that same source, 54-55.
[2] The contrast is between the social, or collective, life and the individual('s) life.

much, by the *notorious* laws of conscience,[3] a man must devote to the first and may give to the second? Are the demands of those who are single legitimate? What are the relations and the balance between the external and the inner life in the most enlightened countries, and what in Russia? I would like to see these questions considered and resolved by you. I need your help in connection with my relations with Širjaev.[4] Two months have passed already, and I have received no proof-sheets. I surmise that for the sake of speed he has decided to publish by my manuscript, not troubling about the fact that I may make certain corrections. In any case I am sending you a copy of "Eda" and "The Feasts", which I corrected long ago, but which are only now ready for dispatch. The proof of this is that moral indolence by which I have for some time been possessed. I am also sending you an introduction in verse to the new edition and a title-page with a musical epigraph. I am hoping that Širjaev will agree to publish an engraving or lithograph of this sheet. He can show me that indulgence in return for the extra poem that I am sending him. I embrace you and send my regards to all your people.

E. Baratynskij

I hope your mother and brother[6] are well now. We, too, have had severe infections all winter, and we all caught pneumonia one after the other.

³ Lit. 'by the laws of notorious conscience'; a second possible reading is: 'by the laws of a certain (i.e. one individual's) conscience...'
⁴ Baratynskij refers to the proof-reading of the collection that eventually appeared in 1835.
⁵ "Vot vernyj spisok vpečatlenij..."; see note 5 to letter 58. The "musical epigraph", too, failed to appear in 1835.
⁶ Petr Vasil'evič Kireevskij (1808-1856), compiler of Russian folk-songs, scholar.

60

To S. L. Èngel'gart   (Early November, 1834; Mara)[1]

Here is a proof-copy for you,[2] my soul. Take a little trouble on my

¹ Taken from *Muranovskij sbornik* (1928), bk. 1, 30. The estate of Muranovo is now no more. The house, however, may be visited. On it, see "Sel'co Muranovo", *Stolica i usad'ba*, 1915, no. 33, 3-8 (heavily illustrated by M. Mazaev), and K. Pigarev, *Muzej-usad'ba Muranovo: putevoditel'* (Moscow, 1963). The original, according to Pigarev in the *1951 edition*, 612, ends with a note to A. L. Baratynskaja, mentioning the coming marriage of E. P. Kindjakovaja with A. N. Raevskij. The marriage, Pigarev notes, occurred on November 11, 1834, on which basis the present letter is based. I have been unable to check the original, which is said to be in *CGALI*.
² A proof-copy of the 1835 collection.

behalf. By the next post I shall send you an epistle to Vjazemskij[3] and an epigram.[4] I forgot my promise completely because of matters concerning the estate. Here is another commission for you. In the 4th chapter of "The Concubine" I intended to erase the final tirade from the line: "Eleckoj, having seen off his guests..." I am rewording it and writing to the press about it, but I'm afraid they won't understand me. Before they send me the proof-copy, glance at it and, if my wish has not been carried out, send it back and tell them to work out what the trouble is. Farewell, I embrace you. Tell me how my corrections strike you.

[3]   "Kak žizni obščie prizyvy", better known as "Knjazju Petru Andreeviču Vjazem-skomu", first appeared not in the collection but in *Sovremennik* (1836), vol. 4, no. 4, 216. Baratynskij sent the piece to Vjazemskij together with the 1835 verse collection. It is a poignant record of the breaking up of the Puškin circle of an earlier decade.

[4]   Structurally speaking, Baratynskij epigrams are of two broad types. First, and especially in the early years (1819-1826), there are epigrams of the type described and approved by Boileau – *un bon mot de deux rimes orné*. Second, there are epigrams of greater length, gracious in form, of the kind developed by Marcus Valerius Martial. Baratynskij interprets 'epigram' in a sense more reminiscent of the Greek Anthology than of eighteenth-century Western verse; satire is certainly no prerequisite (although there are many short, highly polished pieces of a distinctly mordant or even cutting quality). It is possible that the epigram mentioned here is "Xrani svoe neopasen'e", published in the 1835 edition, p. 79, and addressed to an anonymous inmate of the Smol'nyj Ladies' Institute. Another, less likely contender is "Boljaščij dux vračuet pesnopen'e..." There is no conclusive indication that it is either.

61

To N. I. Krivcov   (1834; Moscow)[1]

It was impossible for me to reply to you at the moment of my leaving Mara, the more so because your notice strengthened my own suspicions

[1]   Taken from the original, preserved in the Archive of P. N. and S. N. Batjuškov, Saltykov-Ščedrin Public Library (*rukopisnyj otdel*), reference: F. 52, no. 244.

   Nikolaj Ivanovič Krivcov was born of parents far from rich but of ancient blood (Bolkonskij *uezd*, Orlov *gubernija*, 1791). He was taken to Petersburg by a family friend, S. N. Turgenev (the novelist's father), and enlisted as a *Junker*. He fought in the Napoleonic Wars, lost a leg at Kul'mo, saw his military career shattered and, at the age of 22, embarked on a comprehensive course of education of his own designing. For two years he studied in Geneva and Paris, visiting England briefly. He met Žukovskij, Karamzin and Puškin, La Harpe and Alexander I. He then served in the Russian Embassy in London, under Count Lieven. He became an anglophile and introduced English ways into his household on returning to Russia in 1819. He was appointed Governor of Tula, then of Voronež. On Alexander's death, in 1825, his fortunes broke. He was slandered, retired, and spent his years making "a small oasis" of a barren plain (B. N. Čičerin, *op. cit.*, 511-516). He built an English country house

and gave substance to an anxiety that was at first quite vague. Since arriving here, I have been prey to a horrible anxiety, having found no news from Mara whatever and receiving none for two posts in succession. A letter from Sophie[2] has finally dispelled it, and I feel strong enough to write to you to thank you sincerely for the most true, solicitious friendship that you are showing my brother.[3] Allow me to say to you that he merits it by the profound esteem and tender affection that he has for you – one of those enthusiastic affections of which only noble youth is capable, and which you have the virtue to appreciate. Sophie is deeply touched by all the attentions you lavish on Sergej. The presence of Čičerin, who came at your invitation, has diverted him.[4] You do (–) to bring him to us here. I hope that you are resting. But it is on hearing your voice that he is most tractable. In all events, after all my contrivances(?) the moment of greatest danger is over. His state of melancholic exaltation does not continue long at its most intense, (–)[5] him to fall into dejection, and a dejection that is quite without (–). It is only with considerable uneasiness, however, that I take upon myself the burden of comforting him. You who are present already, you who can observe the every shade of this unhappy illness that possesses Sergej, will not abandon him, you will continue to give him your truly brotherly attentions. Be so good as to present my children to Mme and Mlle Krivzoff[6] and rest assured of, etc.

Sincerely, E. Baratynskij

near Mara, and became the close friend of Sergej Baratynskij (see note 2 to letter 3). Puškin liked and admired him; see *A. S. Puškin, 1962*, vol. 9, 15, 80, 86; vol. 10, 19-20. Having fox-hunted for many years with the Odoevskijs, Čičerins and Baratynskijs, he lowered the flag on his 'English castle' for the last time in 1843.

[2] Sophie Èngel'gardt, the poet's sister-in-law.

[3] Sergej. When he fell ill is uncertain. Čičerin records that he was prone to attacks of acute depression over many years. Baratynskij left Mara in 1832 to build a house at Kajmary, near Kazan'. Thereafter he returned to Mara at irregular and infrequent intervals.

[4] It is thanks to Čičerin's memoirs that anything is known of the social life that was built up, in the 1830s, among the families of Ljubiči, Mara, Osinov'ko in Tambov.

[5] The writing is far from plain. 'Allows him...' would be a logical guess here.

[6] To the letter was adjoined a note to Krivcov's wife. The two letters were sent together. The note reads as follows: "A thousand thanks, Madame, for the extreme kindness that you have had in giving us your news. It appears that the solitude of Ljubiči (*sic*) is more animated than Moscow, the great city. It is now two months since we had the good fortune to enjoy the least chat or the most innocent scandal. Plainly, you are (–) and we have been abandoned by it. I will pray God that He stir up all kinds (–) around you as much as He can, in order that you may recount it to us on your return to Moscow... I commend myself sincerely to your friendship. E. Baratynskij. My wife and my sister wish to be remembered to you."

The note is an interesting indication of Baratynskij's willingness to alter his style to what he thinks fitting in a note to a woman. Elsewhere, there is no evidence that he has much interest in innocent scandal, but a good deal of evidence that he would prefer, when possible, to avoid both scandal and chat. He gives Krivcova to understand that she is fortunate to be "in the thick of things"; yet he prefers not to live in Moscow himself.

These two letters illustrate Baratynskij's affection for Krivcov and his wife, and stress the extent of his involvement in local Tambov society, especially, and naturally, with the neighbouring families of Krivcov and Čičerin. They also cast light on the isolation of rural estates in 1834. Mail was slow and the journey to Moscow long. Clearly, however, Baratynskij had no intention of losing contact with Mara, and with the events in it.

62

To P. A. Vjazemskij   (5 February, 1837; Moscow)[1]

I am writing to you under the crushing effect produced on me, and not on me alone, by the terrible news of Puškin's death.[2] As a Russian, as a colleague, as a family man I mourn and am indignant. We have lost a talent of the first order which had perhaps not yet come to its full development, which would have accomplished something unforeseen, had the intrigues that circumstances span for him been dealt with,[3] had fate, in his last, desperate struggle with them, tipped its balance in his favour. I cannot express what I feel. I only know that I am deeply shaken, and ask myself constantly, with murmurs and bewilderment and tears, why was it like this and not otherwise? Is it natural that a great man, of mature years, should perish in a duel like a careless boy? How much was he to blame, how much were others to blame, how much an unhappy predestination? In what sudden movement of ill-will towards the rising voice of Russia did Providence remove its eye from the poet who had long formed Russia's glory and who was still, (say malice and envy what they may), its mighty hope? I informed the father[4] the very minute I learned of the terrible event. He, like a madman, was for a long time unwilling to believe it. Finally, to general and highly unconvincing exhor-

[1] Taken from *Starina i novizna*, 1900, bk. 3, 341-342.
[2] For a dull but factually accurate account of Puškin's duel with d'Anthès, and of the events of the preceding days in January, 1837, see W. N. Vickery, *Pushkin: Death of a Poet* (Indiana, 1968). The duel was ostensibly over the honour of the poet's wife Natal'ja, née Gončarova. Puškin was wounded in the stomach, and died after three days. Tens of thousands flocked to the church in Moscow where his body lay before, in the dead of night, it was taken out and sent to Svjatye Gory, near Mixajlovskoe. Like Vjazemskij and Žukovskij, Baratynskij was deeply shaken.
[3] Or, 'had the nets cast for him been dealt with...'
[4] Sergej L'vovič Puškin (1770-1848), then residing in Moscow.

tations, he said: "One thing remains for me – to pray God not to take my memory away, so that I shall not forget him." This was said with heart-rending tenderness.

There are those in Moscow who have heard of the common disaster with a detestable indifference, but the majority, sympathetic and horror-struck, will soon force them into a decent hypocrisy.

If I have not replied to your letter before this, circumstances which, perhaps, you know already are to blame. I have lost my father-in-law,[5] and his death has transferred many real worries to me. Besides that, I wished to add something for your literary almanac to my letter, and have waited for a moment of leisure and inspiration, but in vain up to the present.

E. Baratynskij

Address: His Grace, the noble lord, Prince Petr Andreevič Vjazemskij.[6] In S(aint) P(etersburg), Moxavoja St., in the house of Admiral Byčinskij's wife.

[5] Lev Nikolaevič Èngel'gardt died, also in Moscow, on November 4, 1836. The "many real worries" were connected with the management of the estate of Muranovo, which passed entirely into the poet's hands.
[6] On translations of official titles, see Introduction. The Vjazemskijs were not Petrine upstarts; the family had been princely in the 14th century; see V. V. Rummel', *Rodoslovnyj sbornik russkix dvorjanskix familij*, 2 vols., vol. 2 (St.P., 1887).

63

To P. A. Vjazemskij   (February, 1837; Moscow)[1]

I am forwarding my tribute to *The Contemporary* to you.[2] On hearing the news of Puškin's death I was working on the last strophes of this poem.[3] Each man works in his own way. A lyrical piece I always throw

[1] Taken from *Starina i novizna*, 1902, bk. 5, 54.
[2] Baratynskij continued to think of his contributions to *Sovremennik*, 1837-1844, as tributes to Puškin's memory. The journal had been founded and edited by Puškin. In 1839 he contributed three poems, in 1840 two, in 1841 three, in 1842 and 1843 one, and in 1844 five. All the pieces that he wrote abroad during the journey to Italy were printed in *Sovremennik*.
[3] "Osen'" was published in *Sovremennik* (1837), vol. 5, no. 1, 279. On this poem, see E. N. Kuprejanova's notes in the *1957 edition*, 371-372. Stanza 14 of the poem is provocative. The 'verb' or 'word' of the penultimate line would seem to be that of the true poet (Puškin or, perhaps, Baratynskij himself), which is ignored, in the romantic tradition, by the crowd (*tolpa*). But who or what is the hurricane? And who gives voice to "common thoughts" in a stupid, banal way?

down more than carelessly, from the very moment of conceit; the verses are sometimes without measure, sometimes without rhymes, but I think only about their movement, and later settle down to the finishing of details. For a long time I left my elegy which, thrown down on paper, was still far from written. I am dissatisfied with a great deal in it now, but am deciding to be indulgent with myself, the more so since the careless points I left are, it appears, acceptable to fate. I commend myself to your memory as a friend.

E. Baratynskij

64

To P. A. Pletnev   (Early in 1839; Moscow)[1]

My dear Pletnev, dear still, as always![2] My relative, Putjata,[3] writes to me that you are angry with me. Thank you for that. Whoever is angry remembers and, perhaps, loves. The poem published in *Notes from the Fatherland*[4] was torn from under my pen by my brother Sergej,[5] whom you have met perhaps, since he is now in Petersburg, – and for that reason it is rather weak stylistically. For a long, long time there has been no contact between us; but for a long, long time I have not written verse, and have left that world in which we once met and drew close to one another. Can you think that I have forgotten the past? What should I remember if not that! But fate, which in my youth removed me from people, from their ways and the conditions of society life, having rewarded me with such friends as yourself, then threw me, inexperienced and long since disenchanted, both into society and into the trivialities of normal life. As a man, I had to learn what children learn, to grasp relationships, to acquire habits, to guess what others know for certain. These last ten years of my life, in no way peculiar at first glance, have been

[1] Taken from *Russkaja starina*, June, 1904, 519-520. Dated on the basis of the reference to "Tolpe trevožnyj den' ...", published in the journal mentioned in 1839, vol. 11, no. 2, 1. On P. A. Pletnev, see note 2 to letter 32.
[2] The two met in 1818 or early 1819.
[3] Sophie L'vovna Putjata, née Èngel'gardt (1811-1884), the poet's sister-in-law.
[4] "Tolpe trevožnyj den'..."; *Otečestvennye zapiski* was founded in 1839 and edited for twenty-one years by Andrej Aleksandrovič Kraevskij (1810-1889), a civil servant of literary bent. Baratynskij contributed "Na čto vy dni!" and "Vsegda i v purpure i v zlate" to it in 1840, and "Predrassudok! on oblomok...", "Čto za zvuki?..." and "Ropot" in 1841. Thereafter his contributions ceased.
[5] See note 2 to letter 3.

harder for me than were all the years of my Finnish incarceration. I grew tired, and lapsed into a state of melancholy. You I did not place on a level with people whom I came to know later; but how am I to start on this long and complicated tale which changed me so profoundly, on new impressions, the gradual growth and interaction of which are unknown to you? How does one give oneself up to a friendship of earlier years?[6] I do not wish to send you lines that are cold, incomplete. Is it not for this reason that old men are taciturn? All this chatter means, in the final analysis; you, your friendship and the memory of the past, are precious to me, and if at any moment it ever seemed to you otherwise, appearances deceived you.

I am sending you a few small poems[7] that I have thrown down this last week.

I am now in the confusion that preparations for a long journey produce. I am travelling with my family to the south shore of the Crimea, where I shall spend about eighteen months. I want sun and rest, a solitude and quiet broken by nothing – infinite if possible. I am thinking of taking up the pen again and, if everything that has accumulated in my mind and lain on my heart finds outlet in expression, hope to be the good servant of *The Contemporary*.

Farewell. I embrace you fondly. Keep your old friendship for me.

E. Baratynskij

[6] Lit. 'of ancient, or bygone, years'.
[7] Those poems that appeared in *Sovremennik* in 1839 (vol. 15, 157-158), under the general heading "Antologičeskie stixotvorenija": "Blagosloven svjatoe vozvestivšij...", "Byli buri, nepogody" and "Ešče, kak patriarx, ne dreven ja..."
The plans for a journey to the Crimea mentioned here were shortly afterwards changed and expanded. It is of interest that the principal reason set forward for the projected journey is a need of sun and rest – not a wish to visit Italy, cradle of Western culture, to broaden his children's outlook, etc. Those factors seem to have impressed themselves on him later.

65

To A. F. Baratynskaja   (Winter, 1840; Petersburg)[1]

Sophie K. is exceedingly kind;[2] she and I immediately grew tolerably

[1] Taken from the *1951 edition*, 528-529, where it is taken from the original. The exact dates of Baratynskij's stay with his brother Iraklij and with the Karamzins are unknown.
[2] Sofija Nikolaevna Karamzina (1802-1856), daughter of the poet and historian. To

intimate; they say that I, too, was very amiable.[3] The Karamzins have a *salon* in the full sense. In the course of the two hours that I passed there, some twenty persons appeared and vanished. Vjazemskij was there, and Bludov came.[4] Vjazemskij reminded him of his old acquaintance with me. He pretended very sweetly that he had not forgotten, saying that we heard "Boris Godunov" for the first time together. This is not true but, of course, I did not contradict him. I forgot to tell you that before going to the Karamzins we heard Sologub's[5] tale "The Tarantas" at Odoevskij's, a tale embellished by the vignettes, full of art and imagination, of a prince Gagarin. The vignettes were a delight, but the tale mediocre. Everyone critized it. I, too, joined the critics, but was more moderate than the others. The argument begun at Odoevskij's was continued at the Karamzins' and was the chief topic of conversation. The next day (yesterday) I was at Žukovskij's, and spent three hours with him in sorting out unpublished poems by Puškin.[6] There are some of amazing beauty, some completely new in form and spirit. All his last poems are remarkable for – what do you think? – their strength and their depth. *What have we done, O Russians, and whom have we buried!* – words of Feofan[7] on the burial of Peter the Great. Several times I felt tears of artistic enthusiasm and bitter regret welling up.

That same day we went to the French theatre, to Princess Abamelik's box.[8] They were playing "The Lady Reader,"[9] and Mme Allen performed;[10] good, but not extremely so. They said she was out of humour, and that someone had offended her behind the scenes. P(rincess) Odoevskaja was sitting in her box alone. Meeting my glance, she beckoned me to her side, and I sat through the entire first act with her. There we spoke of Elagin[11] and Kireevskij. The late evening I passed with my family. There you have not a letter, but a journal. Already I long to return home, although I am passing the time very pleasantly.[12]

---

her, Baratynskij dedicated an eight-line rhymed compliment, commonly known as "S knigoju 'Sumerki' S.N.K." (published in *Sovremennik*, 1842, vol. 27, 95). Baratynskij mentions the salon which he frequented in the winter of 1840.

[3] Here, in an access of modesty on re-reading his letter, Baratynskij heavily crossed out seven lines; they are illegible.

[4] Count Dmitrij Nikolaevič Bludov (1785-1864), minor writer and statesman. Having earlier been a member of the Society of Arzamas, Bludov later repudiated his connections with such men as Orlov and Nikolaj Turgenev; see M. V. Nečkina, (translated into English as) *Russia in the Nineteenth Century* (Ann Arbor, 1952), index under Bludov, D. N.

[5] Count Vladimir Aleksandrovič Sol(l)ogub (1814-1882), minor writer, government servant and courtier. In February 1836, he and Puškin came close to duelling; however, there was a reconciliation two months later (see *A. S. Puškin, 1962*, vol. 10, 405).

[6] Žukovskij was then preparing the first posthumous edition of Puškin's verse.

[7] Feofan Prokopovič (1681-1736), a priest raised to unprecedented heights in the Russian Orthodox Church by Peter the Great. Prokopovič had studied in Italy, was conversant with Western culture and the practice and conventions of baroque oratory, and immortalized himself with a "Slovo pogrebal'noe" (1725), pronounced in Petro-pavlovskij Cathedral on the death of Peter (1725). He was a vigorous, but not ob-scurantist, opponent of the Muscovite version of Byzantinism and of scholasticism, became Peter's chief ecclesiastical adviser and was mainly responsible for a so-called Spiritual Regulation (1721), in accordance with which the Holy Synod was established in place of the Patriarchate and the Church reduced to little more, in practice, than a government department.

[8] Princess Mar'ja Ioakimovna Abamelek, née Lazareva. Iraklij Baratynskij married her daughter Aleksandra in 1835. Through her, Iraklij had entrée to Petersburg high society.

[9] *La Lectrice*; vaudeville by a collaborator or imitator of E. Scribe(?).

[10] Louise Despréaux Allan (1810-1856), French actress, celebrated for her playing of Musset's *Un Caprice* (1847).

[11] Aleksej Andreevič Elagin was I. V. Kireevskij's father-in-law. N. M. Jazykov was also on the friendliest terms with the Elagins; see N. M. Jazykov, *Polnoe sobranie stixotvorenij* (Leningrad, 1964), 327, 388, 371, 659.

[12] A further six and a half lines are erased at the conclusion of this letter. They are illegible. Baratynskij writes with the air of one who, although fully entitled to such diversions as theatrical performances and conversations with the rich and witty, is not accustomed to them. As a new-comer, he is busy meeting people and retailing his news. His wish to return home "although he is passing the time very pleasantly" rings true.

66

To N. V. Putjata   (19 April, 1842; Artemov)[1]

Christ is risen! I wish you a merry festival,[2] which we, for our part, have begun satisfactorily. At three in the morning we attended mass in a neighbouring village, broke our fast and had a good sleep. I am writing to you on Easter Sunday itself.

After a moment of indecision, we have decided to stay put, having in any case (a case that it is hard to foresee, however) a refuge in Moscow and a still nearer one in Troica where, by the way, our mill is situated[3]

[1] Taken from K. Pigarev's *Muranovo* (Moscow, 1948), 138. (The work contains a useful bibliography on the estate and the poet's dealings with it.) Artemovo was the estate of the Pal'čikovs, and was close to Muranovo (forty miles from Moscow). Baratynskij and his family lived with the Pal'čikovs while a new house was being built at Muranovo in 1841-1842. Each day he rode over to inspect the progress. He had himself designed the house; see illustrations in *1936 edition*, vol. 1.

[2] Easter.

[3] One has here a hint at the extent of Baratynskij's commercial activities and entre-preneurial spirit in the fifth decade. It is striking that the commerce, so harmful to literature (in Baratynskij's estimate; see "Primety", "Poslednij poèt"), does not seem

and, consequently, our local office of management, to which, no doubt, the necessary grants have been made in the present circumstances.[4] The wording is splendid.[5] The matter could not have been approached more intelligently or cautiously! Blessed is he who comes in the name of the Lord! The sun is in my heart when I think of the future. I see and feel the possibility of bringing the great cause to fulfilment both quickly and peaceably. Farewell, I embrace you and your babies with all my heart.

E. Baratynskij

Address: His Excellency Nikolaj Vasil'evič Putjata. On the corner of Počtamtskaja St., opposite Isakie, in Kütner's house.

---

to him harmful in other spheres. Distress at the sight of encroaching industry is, of course, a commonplace of Western literature of the romantic period. By 1817, Wordsworth could complain bitterly that "everything has been put up to market and sold for the highest price it would buy" (*The Letters of Wordsworth*, selected by P. Wein, London, 1954, 149). Railways were anathemized by de Vigny; 'the iron age', coined by Hesiod, became a fashionable phrase among the poets of a later aeon (Batjuškov, in "Perevod pervoj satiry Boalo"; Puškin, in "Razgovor knigoprodavca s poètom"). Puškin's poet was persuaded to part with his manuscript. Baratynskij was – theoretically – not so easily persuaded. Yet in 1839, when "Primety" was written, there was little heavy industry in the Russian Empire. Not until 1842, when Baratynskij was leaving the country for ever, did the British repeal on the exporting of machinery allow Knoop, and members of the Russian merchant-manufacturing families, to mechanize the cotton-spinning and weaving industries in Moscow and a small number of other towns (see I. Aksakov, *Issledovanie o torgovle na Ukrainskix jarmarkax*, St.P., 1858 and M. B. Xrapčenko, *Tvorčestvo Gogolja*, Moscow, 1956, 5-11). It is possible to see great threats in small beginnings; but Baratynskij's apprehensions of the ill effect of industry on poetry were an emotional response, and contrast starkly with his practice.

As early as 1835, he had speculated in property, buying a house in Moscow, on Spiridonovka (see *Academy edition*, vol. 1, LXVII-LXVIII). In November 1836 he had taken over the running of the Muranovo estate. By bringing grain from Kazan' and storing it near Moscow, and by selling timber from Muranovo, the poet succeeded in amassing some capital. In 1842 a saw-mill was installed in Muranovo, with a calculated efficiency of 500 logs each 24 hours. This would clear approximately 25 desjatins of forest in a year. He purchased a brick factory. He changed his serfs to the *obrok* system (quitrent in place of the traditional corvée). He was, in other words, a tolerably astute capitalist; see *1936 edition*, vol. 1, CIII-CV. Part of the money raised went on providing for his children, part on the journey through Germany, France and Italy, and part, had it sufficed (which it did not) was to have provided the family with a home in Petersburg on their return.

[4] The reference is to an *ukaz* or decree, promulgated on April 2, 1842, by which landowners might 'free' serfs and provide them with allotments. In return, the serfs would owe certain duties (*objazannosti*) to their former lords. The results of the edict which, naturally enough, caused tremors in reactionary and liberal circles alike, were negligible.

[5] The wording is splendid, it seems, because of the caution inherent in it. However, Baratynskij's attitude towards the question of emancipation, which he saw to be

eventually necessary, was intelligent. He appreciated that the matter rested on the acceptance of certain mutual rights and obligations by ex-serfs and ex-landowners alike; see *Tatevskij arxiv*, 82.

The problem of Baratynskij's definitive attitude towards serfdom, as an institution, has exercised critics and commentators for one hundred and twenty years. All evidence suggests that, while he was well-disposed to the idea of emancipation, Baratynskij took no active measures to make that idea fact. According to N. V. Putjata, "the question (of serfdom) constantly occupied his mind" (writing on Baratynskij in *Russkij arxiv*, 1867, bk. 2, 281-282); further, "in conversations with me (i.e. Putjata – GB) he expressed the view that emancipation should not be brought about otherwise than with a strip of land in the possession of the serfs, landowners being compensated by a financial operation – but of what kind, he would add, he did not take it on himself to indicate..." P. Kičeev, more modest and perhaps more objective in his views although less close to Baratynskij, records that "his most sincere hope was – for the emancipation of serfs on private estates"; "Ešče neskol'ko slov o E. A. Baratynskom", *Russkij arxiv* (1868), bk. 2, 869. Certainly, the lot of serfs on privately owned estates had for centuries been harder than that of crown peasants, thousands of whom, particularly in the north, were almost independent peasant cultivators. It is interesting that Baratynskij should have had political discussions with D. N. Sverbeev, with whom his relations were cordial rather than close. In a letter of December 1830 he wrote to Sverbeev, "you and I had many political discussions, and I would very much like to renew them, the more so because, reflecting on my own, I have changed many of my opinions for yours". This letter is the more interesting for Vjazemskij's reminiscence that internal politics did not concern Baratynskij (see *P. A. Vjazemskij, 1883*, vol. 8, 290-291).

Even in a camp so moderate as G. Lutkovskij's Kjumen', it is improbable that Baratynskij witnessed no harshness (see *Academy edition*, vol. 1, LIV). Zakrevskij's reputation for liberalism was not untarnished. On the infamous 'Pavlov affair', in which N. F. Pavlov (1803-1864) was held for days in a pit dug in the ground, see N. Barsukov, *Žizn' i trudy M. P. Pogodina*, vol. 12, 443-449. It was seen that Baratynskij could speak calmly enough of a starving peasantry when they attacked "the houses of their masters"; yet that he was aware of his own obligations towards his serfs, and purchased grain to feed them in a time of semi-famine. In summary, his attitude typified that of a broad sector of the educated Russian gentry of the second and third decades of the century. Liberal by inclination, his willingness to act at personal sacrifice to help the peasantry, or to upset the social and political *status quo*, was, after 1825 at least, non-existent.

67

To A. F. Baratynskaja   (Summer, 1842; Artemovo)[1]

Your praises of my book,[2] dear and good Mother, are the most delightful and flattering that I have ever received. But I relished them with all the naïveté, all the common sense of pleasure, of which I am capable. At the present moment I am very far from literary inspiration, but welcome from

[1] Taken from *Tatevskij arxiv*, 62-63. The original is in French.
[2] *Sumerki* appeared late in May, 1842.

afar the time when my building[3] will be finished, when I shall have fewer
real cares (there will not, perhaps, be the imagined rest), but which smiles
at me when I think of resuming my former occupations. You understand,
of course, that I shall settle in the country for a fairly long time. My
strenuous activity comes, in essence, only of a great need for rest and
peace. At present our house greatly resembles a small university. There
are five outsiders with us, in one of whom chance has provided us with an
excellent drawing master. Our unextravagant way of life and the income
that we hope to draw from forestry[4] allow us to do a great deal for the
children's education, while they and their teachers enliven our solitude.
This autumn a pleasure awaits me that is new to me – the planting of
trees.[5] We have a good, old gardener who loves his work [6] and I am
counting on his good advice. Farewell, dear Mother. I kiss your hands
tenderly, as do your grandchildren.

[3]   The new house at Muranovo; for details of the plans, see K. Pigarev, *Muranovo*
(Moscow, 1948); see also introductory notes to letter 66.
[4]   See note 3 to letter 66. Baratynskij took the forestry operation very seriously. The
saw-mill installed in 1842 was imported from the West. The countryside around Muranovo is still heavily wooded with birch and pine.
[5]   The planting inspired "Na posev lesa", first published in *Včera i segodnja* (1846),
bk. 11, 68-69. The trees were, in fact, planted in the autumn of 1842 – not in the spring,
as the poem has it. For a short exposition of the piece in the context of the poet's life,
see Pletnev's letter to Ja. K. Grot, *Perepiska Ja. K. Grota s P. A. Pletnevym*, 2 vols.,
vol. 2 (St.P., 1896), 728-729. Baratynskij alludes to his earlier rupture with the col-
laborators on *Moskvitjanin*.
[6]   Baratynskij foresaw that old man in "Rodina" (1821), 11.33-36.

68

To N. V. Putjata   (October, 1843; Paris)[1]

Friends, sisters, I am in Paris![2] and thanks to Sobolevskij,[3] to whom I
shall shortly be writing separately, thanks to his serviceable friendship, I
am seeing not only its buildings and boulevards, although the first glance

[1]   Taken from the original, preserved in the Baratynskij Archive, *CGALI*. Baratynskij
and his wife and elder children (which ones were left with grandparents and with the
Putjatas is not known) left Petersburg for Germany, by carriage, in the autumn of
1843. From Leipzig, they travelled to Berlin by train; thence, they continued their
journey to Paris, arriving in the first week of November; see *Academy edition*, vol. 1,
LXXXIV-LXXXIX.
[2]   The opening line of a light piece by Ivan Ivanovič Dmitriev (1760-1837), "Putešestvie
N. N. v Pariž i London", written, rather cruelly, in the person of Vasilij Puškin.
[3]   Sergej Aleksandrovič Sobolevskij (1803-1870) was a lifelong friend of Puškin, a wit,

at Paris's exterior[4] amply rewards the labours of the distant traveller. I have already called in at the Faubourg St-Germain and seen a few men of letters, but the most remarkable thing in France, in my opinion, is the populace itself, friendly, intelligent, cheerful and full of respect for the law, all the importance, all the social use of which it understands. In Berlin I was amazed at the order in the town, at the precise indisputable nature of people's attitudes. How I marvelled, then, on finding the same thing but in a higher degree in teeming Paris, in its narrow streets, with its endless buying and selling. In Germany one senses a certain murmuring still against the laws of social order that are obeyed; here, people belonging to the lowest rabble take a pride in them. Certain clear notions of community have become the common property, and form such a mass of common sense that it is hard to believe it would be possible to lead the people astray from the path of their own true welfare. However, the parties are agitating. I hear a great deal and read a great deal. Those who stand out from the mass, and who fill the newspapers and *salons*, are not firm in their opinions. Here, turncoats are less to be scorned than at first glance it appears, and many of them adopt an opinion contrary to that which they expressed earlier with perfectly sincere empty-headedness. The question of education is occupying everyone now:[5] who should manage it, the Church or the University? The question is extremely important and merges with some aspects of the question of legitimism. Lamartine has published a rubbishy diatribe,[6] which I am constrained to praise in the society with which I have formed an acquaintance. The replies of the opposing party, deferential to the poet's talent, are most amusing. The professors have begun their courses and no matter what they speak about, anatomy or chemistry, manage to touch on the question occupying everyone. We are living in the very centre of the city. Here is our address: Rue Duphot, near the Boulevard de la Madeleine, no. 8.[7] Today I shall be at Mme Aguesseau's,[8] tomorrow at Nodier's,[9] the following day at Thierry's.[10] For all these acquaintanceships I am indebted to the Circourts.[11] Farewell, I embrace you and the children. My warmest regards to Sobolevskij and Pletnev. I see A. I. Turgenev, who is now a little unwell, almost every day. He reproaches Vjazemskij for not writing to him. Remind him of me. I see Balabin,[12] a most intelligent and knowledgable man, to whom I am drawn closer each time we meet.

---

writer of epigrams and traveller. A brief glance at the index of any edition of Puškin's correspondence illustrates the closeness of Puškin's relationship with Sobolevskij; see also V. I. Saitov, *S. A. Sobolevskij, drug Puškina* (Petrograd, 1923). Sobolevskij had received an education based on the precise sciences, but was widely read in several literatures and had connections in numerous European cities. He was, as the present letter makes plain, kindly; he also had an excellent memory, reciting verse by Puškin by heart in 1855; see V. Nabokov, *op. cit.*, vol. 3, 362. Sobolevskij's letters, as this letter also shows, saved the poet a great deal of time and effort.

[4]   Lit. "the first material glance at Paris". A Gallicism, and far from clear. Possibly, "the first real glance..."

[5]   The question was acute by 1843, and Saint-Germain was the centre and fortress of the Church party (ecclesiastical and legitimist causes still being intimately linked in the France of Louis-Philippe). Attacks on the University, however, brought forth the anger of such men as Michelet and Cousin.

[6]   Alphonse Lamartine (1790-1869), a legitimist in 1842, later threw in his lot with the republicans. His political career was ended suddenly in 1848.

[7]   The house is not standing.

[8]   La marquise d'Aguesseau, a grand-daughter of Henri-François d'Aguesseau (1668-1751), orator, courtier under Louis XIV, and Chancellor of France (1727-1750).

[9]   Charles Nodier (1780-1844). Baratynskij informed his mother that he "had caught him among the living". The day after his conversation with the French poet, Nodier fell seriously ill (see *1869 edition*, 515). Hugo, Vigny, the Ancelots and the Deschamps had frequented Nodier's Sundays in l'Arsenal in 1823; see M. Braunschvig, *Notre Littérature Etudiée dans les Textes* (Paris, 1937), 427-30. On Baratynskij's coming to Paris, Nodier was an aging and venerable figure.

[10]   Which Thierry, Augustin (1795-1856), or Amédée (1797-1873), is not known. On the two historians, the latter of whom is rightly overshadowed by the former, see M. Braunschvig, *op. cit.*, 632-633, 649-650.

[11]   Le comte Adolphe de Circourt (1801-79), French *littérateur*, and his wife, the Russian-born Marija-Anastasija de Circourt, née Xljustina (1813-1863). The Circourts were friends of P. Ja. Čaadaev, and Xljustina the authoress of several articles on Russian literature, notably of a lengthy study published in *Bibliothèque de Littérature Universelle*, November, 1829. It was at the request of the Circourts that Baratynskij undertook the prose translation of some twenty of his own poems (see *Academy edition*, vol. 1, 191-199). His work had already been translated into French, however; in 1837, Paul de Julvécourt had rendered "Razuverenie" (somewhat idiosyncratically) as "Marie" (see *Drevnjaja i novaja Rossija*, May 5, 1880, 26). In 1838 Ancelot (who had visited Russia and subsequently published *Six Mois en Russie; Lettres Ecrites à M. X-B. Santine en 1826 à l'Epoque du Couronnement de Sa Majesté l'Empereur*, Paris, 1827), had tried his hand at translation, and produced "Čerep" in prose (M. Ancelot, *Oeuvres Complètes*, 1838, 556). Then there had been Karolina Pavlova's French version of *Das Nordlicht – Les Préludes*, (Paris, Didot frères, 1839). There had, of course, been Russians in Parisian *salons* since 1814; Baratynskij was acquainted with A. I. Turgenev, N. A. Mel'gunov (1804-1867), Žukovskij and Sobolevskij, all of whom, like the Ancelots and the Circourts, formed links between Russian and French literature. In the winter of 1843, Baratynskij met another human link – Mérimée; see my article "E. A. Baratynskij and Prosper Mérimée", *Romance Notes*, XI (1970), no. 3, 531-535.

[12]   Evgenij Petrovič Balabin, Russian diplomat in Paris.

69

To N. V. Putjata   (Early December, 1843; Paris)[1]

It is good that I am only spending one winter in Paris, otherwise from being a person with *some* sense I should become a perfect idler and, what is worse, a society man. Not only I but all Parisians pass the hours in visiting, and are on their feet from eleven in the morning until twelve at night. For true Parisians, having both business and political prospects and visiting each individual with a certain object, this life is not completely killing; but for the visitor, curiosity notwithstanding, it is exhausting in the extreme. Despite the general affability and the novelty of what you see, you feel a lack of straightforward relations, and were I in Paris without my family I do not know if I could endure such an existence. My first acquaintances drew me into the Faubourg St-Germain, to Mme de T's, to Mme d'Aguesseau's, to T's[2]. There, academicians and Catholic proselyters of both sexes gather. All this serves as a Lord's vineyard, in the abbés' sense of the phrase. In the famous suburb's rather secluded streets, latin priests with preoccupied expressions run in such numbers that, were one to spit on meeting every one in the Russian manner,[3] one might grow consumptive. Circourt has introduced me to de Vigny,[4] the two Thierry, Nodier, St-Beuve,[5] Sobolevskij to Mérimée[6] and Mme Ancelot,[7] and chance to the former editor of one of the extreme republican journals, through whom I hope to come to meet G. Sand.[8] I have met or renewed my acquaintance with several fellow-countrymen.[9] In Paris,

[1] Taken from the original, preserved in the Baratynskij Archive, *CGALI*.
[2] Presumably, Thierry; two lines are crossed out here.
[3] It was a custom in European Russia before the Revolution, and in the *Pribaltika* until the last years of the 19th century, to spit over one's left shoulder on meeting a priest in the street – the priesthood seemingly representing death.
[4] Alfred de Vigny (1799-1863).
[5] Charles-Auguste Saint-Beuve (1804-1869), poet and critic.
[6] See conclusion of note 11 to letter 68.
[7] Madame Ancelot received numerous visiting Russians in her *salon*.
[8] Baratynskij misspells Sand as Zand. Lucile-Aurore Dudevant, née Dupin (1804-1876), was best known in Russia as the author(ess) of the novels *Indiana* (1832), *Lélia* (1833), *Mauprat* (1837) and *Consuelo* (1842-1843). To Baratynskij, she was first of all the authoress of personal and lyrical works; not until 1837 did the influences of Lamennais and Pierre Leroux begin to make themselves felt on her work (with the socialist and humanitarian *Spiridion* (1839)). By 1843, her views were republican; therefore Baratynskij hoped to meet her through "the former editor of one of the extreme republican journals". He was methodical in his approach to distinguished writers.
[9] Nikolaj Turgenev (1789-1871) was in Paris. So, too, were several *personae non*

and in foreign parts in general, Russians seek out Russians. The most thoughtless of them divine what is in our heart and are ready for sentimentality. From the political viewpoint, the societies present the saddest of spectacles. Intelligent without hope, reckless through incorrigible habit, the legitimists pursue the idea of their party and have celebrated an apt and moving requiem for it in London. The republicans, without a single practical idea, lose themselves in theories. The conservative party almost hates its present representative, the king chosen by it.[10] Everywhere there are elements of discord. The movement of the priests rises to calamitous prospects, for under the guise of mysticism they pursue the idea of regaining their former sway. There is France! But in the *salons* of Paris the French constitution of civility peaceably brings together intelligent, powerful, passionate representatives of all these various aspirations. I embrace you both and all your children and ours. In my next letter I will give you details about all those I have mentioned.

---

gratae in Benckendorff's Russia – the minor poet Nikolaj Mixajlovič Satin (1814-1873), the publicist and memoirist Ivan Gavrilovič Golovin (1816-1884), and Nikolaj Ivanovič Sazonov (1815-1872). All were acquainted with Herzen and Ogarev, and of a younger generation than Baratynskij, whom they respected as a former friend and colleague of Puškin and a victim of Alexandrine oppression. There is no doubt whatever that the Russian *émigrés* saw Baratynskij in a far more radical light than facts warranted. He was "a warrior... felled by tsardom"; "he left us", N. Satin recorded, "with many plans, charging us to bring them to fulfilment" (see L. G. Frizman, *Tvorčeskij put' Baratynskogo*, Moscow, 1966, 126-128). Certainly, while in Paris he heard "a highly effective speech" by Golovin, in which serfdom was roundly condemned (*ibid.*, 126, and E. Bobrov, *Dela i ljudi*, Jur'ev, 1907, 171). Since he had himself given the dinner at which Golovin spoke, moreover, he was not present by chance. But that he should have given such a dinner in Petersburg in 1840 is inconceivable. The incident is isolated.
[10]   *La partie de la résistance*, headed by Guizot, was then in power. *La partie du mouvement* formed the turbulent opposition. Representatives of the latter were Odilon (1791-1873) and Lafitte. The hated king was Louis-Philippe (1773-1850), scorned, in varying degrees, by high society in Paris, Petersburg and London. His reign extended from 1830 to 1848.

70

To N. V. Putjata   (Late December, 1843; Paris)[1]

Dear friends, I wish you a happy new year and embrace you, your children and ours; I wish you a better one than this one in Paris, which is nothing but a spectre of the past, wrinkled and in holiday dress. I con-

---

[1]   Taken from *Russkij arxiv*, 1867, bk. 2, 289-290.

gratulate you on the future, for there is more of it with us than anywhere;[2] I congratulate you on our steppes, for that is a space for which the sciences of Western Europe will never find a substitute; I congratulate you on our winter, for it is bracing and brilliant, and the eloquence of its frost calls us to action better than the orators of the West; I congratulate you on our being, indeed, twelve days younger than other peoples, for which reason we shall perhaps survive them by twelve centuries. Each of these phrases I can prove in a scientific manner; but now there is no time, let us leave that until the day when we meet, for of all Russian writers there is not one who cares less to write than he who loves you so well.[3] My greetings to Sobolevskij and to Pletnev, to whom I am preparing to write, not knowing what about, such is the complexity of the subject; but I will try to express *something* with all the justness that lies in my power.

E. Baratynskij

[2] Distance from Russia seemingly weakened Baratynskij's appreciation of its blacker aspects, heightened his patriotism and, by extension (in a radical *milieu*), increased a latent desire for action on the political front. There is no comparable patriotic outburst elsewhere in his verse or correspondence.
[3] I.e., Baratynskij himself.

71

To N. V. Putjata   (Spring, 1844; Paris)[1]

Sonečka's[2] last letter brought us the news of your great common loss. You will not doubt of the fullness of the sympathy that we feel. The memory of your respected father[3] belongs not to your filial grief alone but to all who knew and esteemed him; it belongs to history, to the civil history of 1812.[4] You are passing a hard winter: so many emotional upheavals, so many real anxieties. My life here, too, is not exquisite. I shall be content with Paris when I leave it. For the foreigner participating passionately in nothing, for the cold observer, social duties, which feed only a curiosity often deceived in its expectations, are extremely weari-

[1] Taken from *Russkij arxiv* (1867), bk. 2, 290-292.
[2] Sophie L'vovna Putjata.
[3] Vasilij Ivanovič Putjata died on December 4, 1843.
[4] V. I. Putjata had supervised the building of field-hospitals during the Napoleonic Wars and campaigns of 1813-1815 and was responsible for the fitting-out of Russian reserves and troops abroad. He was a military administrator, not a soldier.

some. I attend everywhere necessary, like a pupil at his classes. A mass of information and impressions reward my labour of course, but still it is labour and only very rarely pleasure. In one of Vjazemskij's letters to Turgenev there are some lines that are particularly kind in my regard. Tell him, when you have the chance, that I was very touched by them and that they are preserved in that faculty that has so well been called memory. Poor Turgenev has been ill practically since my arrival: he has sciatica in the hand and rheumatism in his sides. By his account, he is indebted for these ailments to the fact that, seeking out Žukovskij somewhere in Germany, he fell into a stream, caught a chill and has since then been unable to recover. He does not leave his armchair, and for a man as active as he that is worse than illness itself. In the evenings we ride through the F(aubourg) St-Germain, faithful, in the meanwhile, to the Orthodox Greco-Russian Church. The Catholic proselyting here is insufferable. They have forced me to read a pile of boring books, and now I have lying on my desk *The Order of Jesuits* by father Ravignan.[5] What do you imagine that is? An exposition of the statutes of the order written, with an infant's simplicity or the innocence of an old man who has lost his memory, by a man of forty, remarkable for his learning and his gifts. Here is my definition of this work: *A foolish book, written for the foolish by a man who is not foolish.* I see almost all the authors here. Tomorrow I shall be at Lamartine's. Thierry[6] promised to introduce me to Guizot. Since he has been a minister, access to him has been rather difficult. I have letters to Pletnev and Sobolevskij started but not finished, because of the bustle of Paris. I send greetings to them both. Yesterday Nasten'ka[7] and I attended a ball of the old nobility[8] and saw the entire French aristocracy in all its splendour. Keep well, I embrace you both and the children.

[5]   Like Lacordaire (1802-1861) and l'Abbé de Frayssinous (1765-1841), the Jesuit father de Ravignan (1795-1858) was a representative of that revival of Church oratory that occurred under the Restoration and, especially, under the July Monarchy. The work referred to, *De l'Existence et de l'Institut des Jésuites* (1844) is, indeed, written in a simple style; but Ravignan's was a considered simplicity. He wrote not for theologians but for laymen. It was, however, an extraordinary choice of book for a visiting Russian poet.
[6]   Probably Augustin Thierry, with whom Guizot, as Minister of Foreign Affairs, entrusted the collection of documents relating to the history of the third estate. Guizot's appointment was made in 1840. He held it until the revolution of 1848, which his extreme conservatism did much to provoke.
[7]   A. L. Baratynskaja, the poet's wife.
[8]   The nobility of 1788.

72

To N. V. Putjata   (Early spring, 1844; Paris)[1]

Thank you for requesting my portrait. It is a pity that I have received your letter immediately before our leaving for Italy. However, I will try to satisfy your friendly whim in Paris where, so you write, it is possible to lithograph several copies. If I do not succeed (for time is short), I will put it off until Rome.[2] We shall leave Paris with the most pleasant impressions. Our acquaintances here have shown us so much kindness, so much friendship, that they have healed old wounds.[3] We have been given letters of recommendation for Naples, Rome and Florence.[4] There, as here, we shall be able, if we wish, to make the acquaintance of society; but it seems that we shall not find time to do so. There are people in Paris whom we are leaving even with sadness. The traveller must be a traveller: he should prolong his stay nowhere if he wishes truly to enjoy his misanthrope's happiness. We are leaving for Marseilles; thence, by sea, directly to Naples, from there by land to Rome and so on, and we shall return to Russia via Vienna. I shall meet you rich in memories of every kind. I have grown tired of the Parisian life, but now, on parting with it, am content with the past. I have ceased to write to you about Paris proper because my opinion has changed every day. Moreover, one needs to have been born in Paris to find leisure for thinking and written expression of one's thoughts amidst Paris's distractions and demands. A Russian sees, and cannot believe, that the learned men here lead the very same life, while constantly widening their knowledge and publishing some book or other every year. I embrace you, my dear friends, as I do your children and ours. Although it is good to be abroad I long for my return to the motherland. I want to see you and to chat about foreigners in the Russian manner. Balabin sends you his regards. He is intelligent, kind, informed and obliging.

---

[1] Taken from the original, preserved in the Baratynskij Archive, *CGALI.*

[2] Baratynskij did not keep his promise, and Putjata received no portrait. Nor did he ever see the poet again.

[3] An allusion to Baratynskij's break, in 1836-1837, with Muscovite writers, notably M. P. Pogodin, S. P. Ševyrev, D. N. Sverbeev and Kireevskij. These and others were connected with *Moskvitjanin.*

[4] Baratynskij never saw Florence.

73

To N. V. Putjata   (April-May, 1844; Naples)[1]

We have been fifteen days in Naples, but it seems as though we have been living here a long time, such has been the number of similar, but ever new, impressions. In three days, as though on wings, we were transported from the complex social life of Europe to the luxuriantly vegetative life of Italy, – Italy, which for all its merits ought to be shown on the map as a special part of the world, for it is truly neither Africa nor Asia nor Europe. Our three-day crossing will remain one of my most delightful memories. I escaped sea-sickness. In the leisure that feeling well afforded me I did not leave the deck, but watched the waves day and night. There was no storm but, as our French sailors called it, very heavy weather,[2] consequently liveliness without danger. Among those in our compartment who did not suffer were a very amiable Englishman, two or three insignificant persons, a Neapolitan music teacher,[3] Nikolen'ka[4] and I. We whiled away the time in the intimacy of wartime comradeship. At sea, the fear of something threatening, even though not every day, and shared sufferings or the presence of suffering for a moment, bind people as if there were no such thing as Moscow or Parisian society. On the ship at night I wrote down a few verses[5] which, having altered them slightly, I will send to you and ask you to give to Pletnev for his journal.[6]

Here is Naples![7] I rise early. I hurry to open my window and drink in the bracing air. We have settled in the Villa Reale, above the bay, between two gardens. You know that Italy is not rich in trees; but where there are trees they are wonderfully beautiful. As our northern forests, in their romantic beauty, their pensive undulations, express all shades of melancholy, so the bright green, sharply defined leaves of the trees here capture

[1]   Taken from the original, preserved in the Baratynskij Archive, *CGALI*. The exact date is unknown; Baratynskij arrived in Italy in April 1844. Attempts to identify the steam-packet company by which Baratynskij sailed from Marseilles have proved unsuccessful.

[2]   *Très gros temps.*

[3]   *Maestro* may have ironical overtones; but Baratynskij is not prodigal of irony.

[4]   Nikolaj Evgen'evič Baratynskij (1836-98), the poet's youngest son.

[5]   "Piroskaf" introduced an entirely new note into Baratynskij's verse. It breathes the spirit of optimism – an optimism inspired by the accomplishment of an old ambition and the prospect of seeing Italy, "the earthly Elysium", within hours. Pletnev duly published the piece in *Sovremennik* (1844), vol. 35, no. 8, 215, with the words: "Sredizemnoe more. 1844". A phase in Baratynskij's literary career which might well have resulted from his exposure to the West was cut short by his death.

[6]   Baratynskij thought of *Sovremennik* as 'Pletnev's journal'.

all degrees of happiness. Now the town has woken up: on a mule, in the fresh green of the Italian hay speckled with crimson flowers, a Neapolitan rides at an easy pace, half-naked but in a red hat; that is not a rider but one of the blessed. His face is cheerful and proud. He trusts in his sun, which will never leave him without support.

Twice every day, in the morning and late in the evening, we go down to the marvellous bay, gaze and never tire of gazing. On Chiaja Boulevard, of which we see an imitation in our Moscow one, there are several statues lit up for us now by the Italian moon, now by the Italian sun. I understand artists for whom Italy is necessary. This light that shows up, but without the sharpness of a lamp, all shades, the whole picture of the human form in all the exactness, all the softness of which the artist dreams, is found only here, beneath this wonderful sky. Here, only here, can both the graphic artist and the painter be formed.

We have inspected some of the places near here. We have seen what can be seen at Herculaneum; we have been to Pozzuoli and seen the Temple of Sarapis;[8] but what is entrancing here is that inner life that invests the sky and the air. If the sky beneath which Philomen and Baucis were turned into trees is not inferior to the sky here, Jupiter was bounteously kind and they jointly blessed.[9]

We shall remain here two or three months. In the course of our sea crossing Nasten'ka's nervous rheumatism returned, with a constant pain in the stomach. One of the best local doctors, whom Princess Volkonskaja[10] recommended to us, has urgently prescribed sea baths and the local mineral water.[11] All this will pass off and is nothing to us. With Xljustin,[12] whom a sudden illness has detained in Königsberg, I was expecting to receive a business letter from you. Repeat the data that you have so that I may deal with my affairs. I have no credit in Naples. Be so good as to send me a further 5000 in notes to Naples and to the other towns through which we shall have to pass, supposing that we return to Russia through Vienna. I embrace you fondly, as I do all your children and ours.

E. Baratynskij

[7]   Tantalizingly little is known of the Baratynskijs' stay in Italy, and what is known is largely drawn from this and the following letter. It is quite obvious that the poet was content in Italy. Life there was "sweet". Baratynskij had been told of Italy, its history and culture, by Giachinto Borghese; see "Otryvki iz poèmy 'Vospominanija'" (1820). It was the colourful and exotic that Borghese remembered in the north, but Baratynskij, as is plain here, was in no way disappointed by the reality of Naples. Both past and present capture his attention. He visits the Coliseum and St. Peter's Cathedral like a dutiful but unusually well-informed tourist ("Djad'ke-Ital'jancu", 1844). Places connected with Virgil and Cicero are viewed with almost religious reverence. But he also

sees, and is delighted by, the Italian populace. Italy, like Greece, remains a splendid fiction to him – even after he has seen it.
[8] See note 9 to letter 74.
[9] See Ovid (*Metamorphosis*, VIII, 610-715); the elderly couple Philomen and Baucis hospitably entertained Zeus and Hermes when others refused the gods. The gods then flooded the land, and Philomen's and Baucis's hut was transformed into a temple. On the request of the old couple, they died simultaneously; they were turned into trees.
[10] Zinaida Aleksandrovna Volkonskaja (1792-1862) left Petersburg for Italy in 1829; see "K Z. A. Volkonskoj".
[11] Lit. 'iron water'.
[12] Semen Semenovič Xljustin (1810-1844), related to the Circourts by marriage (see note 11 to letter 68), was a common acquaintance of Puškin, Baratynskij and Putjata. Xljustin's relations with Putjata as a businessman, however, are unknown.

74

To N. V. Putjata   (Late June, 1844; Naples)[1]

We have received several of your letters at once because we thought to send to Rome and Florence to instruct them to send the letters on to Naples. Circumstances are obliging us to stay here far longer than we proposed, and instead of at the end of August we shall hardly be able to return to Russia before the end of November. I would ask you to manage the estate for me. So far as I remember, the dates of payments to the Council of Trustees on my Tambov estate[2] are in June and July, and two of last year's receipts I left with you, friend Putjata. You must pay in a half on those. Dmitrij[3] has the receipts for Nastja's estate; payment date for all of them is October; on those we must pay in one third, which he can do, by my calculation, with the income from the house;[4] but I do not know how the rents are standing, so you must take the business of direction on yourself. The main thing comes last. On leaving the country, I took from a certain Moscow lady, even whose name I do not remember (but Bekker[5] knows her and her private address), a loan of 32,000 at 9 %,

[1] Taken from the original, preserved in the Baratynskij Archive, *CGALI*. This is the latest extant letter by Baratynskij and very probably the last that he wrote. The doctor recommended by Princess Volkonskaja (previous letter) was for Anastas'ja L'vovna, not for Baratynskij himself. Her complaints are mentioned. Baratynskij also felt unwell. His symptoms, however, were ignored. He died, after a short illness, on July 11, 1844; see *1936 edition*, vol. 1, CXV.
[2] Vjažlja (Mara), where the poet was born and passed his first eight years.
[3] Possibly a bailiff – uncertain. "Nastja's estate" was part of Kajmary, near Kazan'.
[4] It seems that Muranovo had been let during the family's absence; to whom and for how much is unknown.
[5] Herman-Heinrich Bekker (Baeker?), the tutor of Baratynskij's children, was entrusted with the running of the Muranovo estate during the family's absence.

which she took in advance. I must repay this private debt, against which all our income for the present year must be used excepting what we owe you and the five thousand that I have asked you to send to us in Naples. Take the balance out of the forest account: it will go towards the payment of your debt to me for the Muranovo house and for the forestry operation.[6] If, as is probable, all that together does not make 32,000, then pay her what is possible; for that you will need to use Bekker.[7] I am sending you two poems.[8] Give them to Pletnev for his journal. In a day or two I shall address letters for him, Sobolevskij and Vjazemskij to you. Please send them on. We are leading the sweetest of existences in Naples. We have already seen all the marvellous places in this area: Pozzuoli, Baia, Castelamare, Sorrento, Amalfi, Salero, Paestum, Herculaneum, Pomneii. For the children our week now passes in lessons, but we make an outing each Sunday,[9] examining local churches, palaces and castles, or simply go to some small village in the countryside. I fondly embrace you both, and your children and ours.

E. Baratynskij

[6]   On Baratynskij's speculation in forestry, see note 3 to letter 66. From the sums mentioned in this letter, it is clear that Baratynskij was very far from poor in the last year of his life. He might well be surprised should the forest and rent yield him 32,000 roubles; for the mortgage of 200 serfs, Puškin received only 38,000 in 1831 (letter to P. A. Pletnev of February 12-16, 1831, *A. S. Puškin, 1962*, vol. 10, 20). Baratynskij himself, it was seen, had done slightly better three years later, receiving 37,000 roubles for 194 souls. The 32,000 roubles in question were certainly in paper currency, but still that would total approximately 9,616 silver roubles at the exchange rate of the day. And in 1831 Puškin had thought 17,000 roubles in currency – less than 5,200 in silver – sufficient for "settling down and a year's living". In 1844, Baratynskij was becoming a tolerably wealthy man.

[7]   Bekker apparently had more charm than Putjata – or would be less embarrassed in discussing monetary details with a creditor and explaining why the debt could not be met immediately.

[8]   "Piroskaf" and "Djad'ke-Ital'jancu". The latter, in which Baratynskij displays both his love of and his deep knowledge of Italy, was his last poem. It was published in *Sovremennik*, 1844, 217-218.

[9]   See note 2 to letter 73. The context suggests that the outings were by horse-drawn carriage.